Changing Tomorrow 3
Grades 9–12

Grades 9–12

Changing Tomorrow 3

Leadership Curriculum for High–Ability High School Students

Linda D. Avery, Ph.D., &
Joyce VanTassel–Baska, Ed.D.

PRUFROCK PRESS INC.
WACO, TEXAS

Prufrock Press Inc.
P.O. Box 8813
Waco, TX 76714-8813
Phone: (800) 998-2208
Fax: (800) 240-0333
http://www.prufrock.com

Table of Contents

Part I
Introduction to the Unit

Introduction
and Overview of the Unit

Rationale

The current clarion call in education to prepare students for the 21st century is an incentive to rethink elements of the curriculum that will best serve the interests of academically gifted and talented learners. One important component of a well-rounded curriculum is the inclusion of a formalized leadership development initiative to ensure these young people acquire the knowledge and skills essential to assuming leadership roles and to practice the habits of mind that will enable them to apply these behaviors in a conscientious and compassionate way. A recent longitudinal study described in the *Harvard Education Letter* concluded that teachers can develop leadership skills in students by allowing them to pursue mastery and success through real-life experiences, rather than relying on rewards such as high test scores and grades (Pappano, 2012). Incorporating such instructional opportunities into the curriculum offerings takes both planning and practice.

Foundations of Contemporary Leadership Development

In the last 20 years, there has been a marked shift in addressing the construct of leadership in our educational system. Traditional models of leadership approached the concept from a hierarchical perspective and to a great extent embedded the teaching of knowledge and skills related to leadership in courses on management and administration, usually reserved for graduate school. This was true in industries such as business, health care, the military, political science, and education itself. In traditional models of leadership, position and rank on the pyramid commanded control, trust was established through transactions, information was guarded and protected, and formal communication channels were used to "message" the mission and strategy (Li, 2010).

More recent understandings of the concept see the opportunity and the need for teaching leadership to individuals for application across a wide spectrum of roles and responsibilities. Open leadership focuses on a shared vision, inspires trust through personal disclosure and authenticity, transforms rather than suppresses conflict, and encourages a perspective that values the long-term impact, not the immediate payoff. The new thinking recognizes that true leadership is an ever-evolving pattern of knowledge, skills, and capabilities that one develops and seeks to perfect over a lifetime of continual learning and reflection.

Changing Tomorrow 3 is designed to draw on some of the most powerful ideas associated with the newest paradigm in leadership development and to help teachers incorporate this knowledge into their curricula for high-ability students at the high school level. Although all learners can benefit from the information and exercises included here, the pacing of the lessons, the emphasis on conceptual thinking skills, and the focus on independent biographical research are best targeted to the abilities and needs of the advanced learner.

Conceptual Strands Underpinning Unit Design

The design of the unit incorporates three conceptual strands:

◎ *Biographical studies*: The unit uses the biographies of six leaders drawn from a cross-section of fields to showcase the abilities, skills, and mindsets correlated with leadership practice. These individual case studies can serve as role models for students. Diversity in gender and race was a factor in their selection as was the level of contribution each has made to date.

◎ *Generalizations about the concept of leadership*: Based on the Taba (1962) Model of Concept Development, the unit is built around eight generalizations about leadership. These generalizations were culled from the theoretical and research base on the construct. Although there are myriad generalizations that can be articulated, the authors crafted these eight with an eye toward their prevalence in the professional literature and their salience for the age of the target population. The generalizations are included in Handout 1.1: Generalizations About Leadership, which is found in Lesson 1.

◎ *Ideas and exercises adapted from contemporary leadership literature*: The unit incorporates ideas and activities that have been adapted from a variety of materials and training guides on how to teach leadership skills. These application exercises have been tailored to high-ability students in high school.

Unit and Lesson Structure

Changing Tomorrow 3 is composed of 10 lessons that address leadership skill development at the high school level for gifted students in grades 9–12. Goals and outcomes for the unit focus on inspiring leadership behaviors, enhancing skills in communication and collaboration, understanding the breadth and complexity of the concept itself, and strengthening metacognitive development. The unit also includes a pre- and postassessment on the concept of leadership that can serve as the basis for measuring student learning gains and instructional effectiveness.

Appendix A contains the Teachers' Rap Sheets, which consist of completed Biographical Charts for each of the leaders studied. They are not intended for distribution to students as they are akin to answer keys, but they will streamline the teacher's preparation process. An annotated bibliography in Appendix B details the scholarship that underpins unit conceptualization, design, and content selection.

The instructional component of the unit is composed of 10 substantive lessons; most lessons are subdivided into four or five parts, resulting in about 35 hours of teaching time across the whole unit. Four of the lessons are overarching in scope. Lesson 1 focuses on the introduction of the concept of leadership itself. Lesson 6 revisits the generalizations about the concept of leadership. Lesson 9 gives a panel of experts the opportunity to dialogue with students about these big ideas and real-world applications. Lesson 10 includes a final synthesis that requires students to integrate information from the individual case studies and to craft an argument to defend or refute the eighth generalization.

Six of the lessons are focused on biographical case studies, and each contains an application of a skill tied to a single generalization. Lesson 2 uses Oprah Winfrey to examine vision. Lesson 3 focuses on Steve Jobs and storytelling, a motivational strategy tied to the second generalization studied. Lesson 4 investigates Dwight D. Eisenhower and team building, also tied to the second generalization. Lesson 5 explores Thurgood Marshall and conflict resolution. Lesson 7 examines the life of Maya Lin and the role of creativity and innovation. Lesson 8 centers on Nikola Tesla and the idea of legacy—how time and history impact a leader's ultimate contributions.

Across the six biographical lessons, there are some common threads. Each lesson begins with the in-class amalgamation of biographical information from the independent research students have conducted as homework. Students are expected to complete a Biographical Chart for each leader studied that requires them to abstract, prioritize, and summarize information on their own. In Part I of the in-class portion of each biographical lesson, students work with the teacher to create a master chart to ensure that there is a common understanding of the important elements of the leader's life. Part II of each of these lessons uses questioning techniques that require students to analyze, evaluate, and synthesize information, linking the leader's biography to the concept of leadership. Part III of each lesson is an application of a task derived from one of the generalizations studied in the unit. Part IV is another set of questions focused on the meta-cognitive skill of self-reflection undertaken through student journal writing.

In addition to the instructional parts, most lessons contain Assessment, Homework, and Extensions sections. Many of the extensions can be substituted for in-class work or homework, but they are primarily designed for independent study for individual students or small clusters of students. Each instructional lesson concludes with templates for student handouts.

Technology Requirements

The unit relies heavily on student access to the Internet to do the biographical research, and some lessons require that videos from the Internet be shown to the class as a component of an instructional activity. Suggested websites are included as starting points for students to begin their Internet research; however, the teacher can select additional sites for students to use as he or she sees fit. The teacher will also need to reproduce the handouts in the unit for distribution to the students.

Adapting the Unit for Local Needs

Like a three-dimensional jigsaw puzzle, the pieces of this unit on leadership interlock to ensure that the goals and outcomes are well covered. However, in education one size does not fit all classrooms. In order to make adjustments that will best suit local school parameters, the authors recommend that teachers first read all 10 lessons. This will reveal how the parts of each lesson tie together and build upon one another as the unit progresses.

If adjustments are needed, here are some ideas for consideration:

◎ The biographical research can be done as an in-class activity. In most instances, this will add another period to the length of the whole lesson. In districts where home access to computers is limited and public libraries are not easily accessible, this adaptation would allow the unit to still be taught. If done as an in-class activity, the number of elements students have to document should be reduced from five to three. (See Part I of Lesson 2 for a description of this option.)

◎ The task requirements for the completion of the Biographical Charts by students can be stratified. The preferred model is that all students complete all assigned elements in the Biographical Chart. If this is too time-consuming and/or too repetitive, students can take responsibility for different elements in the chart. All students should read or view all of the material assigned for the research, but the time allocated to documenting the knowledge regarding a leader's life story can be reduced with this approach.

◎ Journal writing, which is the key instructional strategy typically used in Part IV of the lessons, can be done as homework. Students are asked to select at least two questions to use as prompts, but this can be reduced to one if time is of the essence. Feel free to assign specific questions rather than allowing students to self-select in each and every case.

◎ The questions in Part II are designed to help students connect the biographical information collected to the key ideas about leadership covered in the generalizations and also drawn from the research base on the construct. For instance, there is no specific generalization about initiative, perseverance, and risk taking articulated in the generalizations studied at this level, but these are studied at earlier levels in this leadership series. The questions in Part IV are targeted to meta-cognitive processing (i.e., helping students reflect on the meaning of the material for their own lives and times). However, there is nothing rigid about this organizational pattern. Feel free to mix and match questions from both sections as best fits your instructional needs.

◎ If the content for a given application exercise (usually found in Part III) has already been covered in your curriculum, explore the ideas presented in the section called Extensions for potential substitutions. Also feel free to make your own adaptations throughout the unit.

◎ The unit is designed for consecutive sequencing in the curriculum, and Parts I and II of each lesson should be delivered back to back. However, there can be some spacing between Parts II and III without great loss in instructional continuity.

◎ Rather than eliminating parts of each lesson, you might consider eliminating one whole lesson if necessary. If you do this, try to incorporate the content embedded in the practice exercise for that lesson into one or more of the lessons that you retain. An easy adaptation is to eliminate Lesson 8 on Nikola Tesla. A discussion on the idea of legacy can be tied to Question 7 in Part II of Lesson 7 on Maya Lin. You could also insert Handout 8.2 from the Tesla lesson into Lesson 6. The information accompanying this handout is the only part of the curriculum that talks about the importance of creating ceremonies to celebrate success, a key idea in modern leadership practice. Of course, Tesla is the only true scientist studied, so there is a downside to eliminating his biography from the roster.

◎ The unit can also be taught effectively without requiring the oral and written reports assigned in Lesson 1 and delivered in Lesson 10. If similar task demands are incorporated into other units of study in your local curriculum, there is no need to replicate the same activity here. What is lost if this element of the unit is eliminated is the opportunity for students to see what is gained by reading a real biography of an individual's life, not a web-based digest.

Three Clarifications to Facilitate Unit Implementation

The authors offer three clarifications as a kind of "heads up" in implementing this unit:

◎ There are two sections included on the Teachers' Rap Sheet that are omitted on the student's blank Biographical Chart for each leader studied. The first section is called Lasting Impact and Contributions. In the set of questions provided in Part II of each of the biographical lessons, there is a question asking students to identify these for each leader studied. Students were not asked to document this information as part of the homework because the intent is to get them to think on their feet during class to respond to this prompt. The second section that is omitted on the Biographical Chart is called Death and Aftermath. It was deleted because most of the leaders included in this unit are still alive and, for those who are not, there is not enough material to justify documenting five discrete data points for this element.

◎ The Internet research on the six leaders studied is the primary basis for homework in the unit. In order to help students budget their time for conducting this research, you may want to distribute the full list of leaders studied, the recommended websites, and the due dates for completion of the Biographical Charts at the end of the first class session. This will ensure that students have plenty of time to complete the homework before each new lesson is started.

◎ There is intentional overlap on some of the Internet sites to which students are directed; their rereading of biographical material is designed to reinforce it in their memory banks. Although students are not tested on these biographical details, they need to have a fairly comprehensive knowledge of each leader's life story in order to construct responses to the questions pondered in the in-class discussions and in journal entries. This overlap also gives students a chance to uncover any errors in the information reported on various sites and to see how information is marketed depending on the source.

Fasten Your Seat Belt

There is an axiom in education that one cannot fully know a subject until one can teach it to others. As you embark on this leadership journey with your students, the authors of this unit want you to feel the excitement that comes from trying something new and the wisdom that accrues from seeing how to make it better the next time through. We have created a road map for your travels, but only you can make the changes in itinerary that will allow your students to explore landmark ideas and experience new vistas. May your own knowledge and understanding of contemporary thinking and practice in teaching leadership for change bloom in the process.

Curriculum Framework:
Goals and Outcomes of *Changing Tomorrow 3*

The following are goals and outcomes of *Changing Tomorrow 3*.

1. To provide role models for young people that will inspire leadership by example as an encouragement to seek and fulfill leadership roles and responsibilities for themselves. Students will be able to:
   o conduct biographical research on leaders using the Internet,
   o identify and evaluate the characteristics and skills of various leaders, and
   o synthesize the factors that contribute to effective leadership, including the talent development process.

2. To develop skills in communication and collaboration to deepen student understanding of the complex demands and challenges of leadership. Students will be able to:
   o develop listening skills that promote their understanding of other perspectives,
   o articulate their ideas in written and oral form, and
   o work individually and in multiple group settings to carry out an agenda or execute a sophisticated task demand requiring more than one person's effort.

3. To understand the construct of leadership as it manifests within and across various fields of human endeavor. Students will be able to:
   o construct a definition of leadership,
   o elaborate on team-building and conflict resolution skills as dimensions of effective leadership, and
   o apply leadership knowledge and/or skills to real-world problem resolution.

4. To develop metacognitive skills that will strengthen leadership capacity-building. Students will be able to:
   o articulate the skill sets and habits of mind of past and present leaders,

- create products that reflect an understanding of leadership expectations,
- apply and assess selected leadership skills in carrying out multilayered task demands, and
- reflect on their own leadership strengths and weaknesses through the creation of a personal profile.

Alignment
of the *Changing Tomorrow* Series With National Standards

In any new curriculum endeavor for gifted learners, it is crucial to show how it responds to the national view of curriculum standards in relevant areas. The following alignment framework shows how the *Changing Tomorrow* units respond to the 2010 NAGC Pre-K–Grade 12 Gifted Education Programming Standards, 21st-century skills (Partnership for 21st Century Skills, 2011), and the Common Core State Standards for English Language Arts (National Governors Association Center for Best Practices & Council of Chief State School Officers, 2010).

Alignment to the NAGC Pre-K–Grade 12 Gifted Education Programming Standards in Curriculum and Assessment

The *Changing Tomorrow* units align to the NAGC Pre-K–Grade 12 Gifted Education Programming Standards in the following ways:

- *Scope and sequence development*: The *Changing Tomorrow* units offer a set of interrelated emphases/activities for use across grades 4–12, with a common format and within a key concept on leadership with interrelated generalizations.
- *Use of differentiation strategies*: The authors used the central differentiation strategies emphasized in the standards, including critical and creative thinking, problem solving, inquiry, research, and concept development.
- *Use of acceleration/advancement techniques, including performance pre- and postassessments, formative assessment, and portfolios*: The authors used all of these strategies as well as advanced research skills to ensure a high level of challenge for gifted and advanced students.
- *Adaptation or replacement of the core curriculum*: The project extends the Common Core State Standards by ensuring that gifted learners master them and then go beyond them in key ways. Some standards

are mastered earlier (e.g., reading and language skills), while others are practiced at higher levels of skill and concept in these leadership units.

◎ *Use of culturally sensitive curriculum approaches leading to cultural competency*: The authors have employed international and American multicultural leaders to ensure that students have an appreciation for the contributions of different cultures to our world today.

◎ *Use of research-based materials*: The authors have included models and techniques found to be highly effective with gifted learners in enhancing critical thinking, text analysis, and persuasive writing. They have also used the questioning techniques found in Junior Great Books and the William and Mary language arts units, both research-based language arts programs used nationally with gifted learners.

◎ *Use of information technologies*: The authors have used biographical research as a central tool for learning in an online environment. They also suggest the use of visual media, computer technology, and multimedia in executing the learning activities developed.

◎ *Use of metacognitive strategies*: The authors have included activities where students use reflection, planning, monitoring, and assessing skills. Each activity includes a journal entry that presses students to reflect on their understanding of leadership.

◎ *Use of community resources*: The units include opportunities for students to learn from a panel of experts or to interview a person central to understanding some aspect of leadership.

◎ *Career development*: Biography is the central reading tool used by the authors for students to learn about an eminent person who has demonstrated leadership skills in a given domain.

◎ *Talent development in areas of aptitude and interest in various domains (cognitive, affective, aesthetic)*: The units present people who have succeeded in various domains of human endeavor. Activities provide multiple opportunities for students to explore domain-specific interests, such as writing, viewing, and oral expression, thus exercising multiple levels of skills in cognitive, affective, and aesthetic areas.

Alignment to 21st-Century Skills

The *Changing Tomorrow* units also include a major emphasis on key 21st-century skills in overall orientation, as well as key activities and assessments employed. Several of these skill sets overlap with the differentiation emphases discussed above in relation to the gifted education standards. The skills receiving major emphasis include:

- ◎ *Collaboration*: Students are encouraged to work in dyads and small groups of four to carry out the research activities, to discuss readings, and to organize information on biographical material.
- ◎ *Communication*: Students are encouraged to develop communication skills in written, oral, visual, and technological modes in a balanced format within each unit of study.
- ◎ *Critical thinking*: Students are provided with models of critical thought that are incorporated into classroom activities, questions, and assignments.
- ◎ *Creative thinking*: Students are provided with models of creative thinking that develop skills that support innovative thinking and problem solving.
- ◎ *Problem solving*: Students are engaged in real-world problem solving in each unit of study and learn the processes involved in such work.
- ◎ *Technology literacy*: Students use technology in multiple forms and formats to create generative products.
- ◎ *Information media literacy*: Students use multimedia to express ideas and project learning.
- ◎ *Cross-cultural skills*: Students read and discuss works and events representing the perspectives of different cultures. They have opportunities to analyze different perspectives on issues.
- ◎ *Social skills*: Students work in small groups and develop the tools of collaboration, communication, and working effectively with others on a common set of tasks.

Alignment to the Common Core State Standards for English Language Arts

In addition to the 21st-century skills listed above, there are other points of integration with important curriculum standards such as the Common Core State Standards (CCSS) for English Language Arts. The units draw deeply on nonfiction literature, predominantly biography, as a basis for biographical study. The units require students to cite textual evidence to support their ideas, to integrate information from multiple sources, and to develop and justify their claims made during in classroom discussion. There is also time dedicated to reflective writing, which helps students develop self-awareness, critical thinking, and intellectual curiosity. Because the standards call for a major emphasis on developing argument, the *Changing Tomorrow* units require gifted and advanced students to analyze data, claims, and warrants in the material they read and to develop arguments on specific issues of leadership based on multiple data sources. As such, the unit is well aligned with the new CCSS.

Part II

Pre– and Postassessments and Rubric

Instructions
for the Assessments

One way to help teachers measure both student learning gains and instructional effectiveness is to use a pre- and postassessment tool. In *Changing Tomorrow 2*, this assessment is based on the students' breadth of understanding of the elements of the concept of leadership using a concept mapping technique. The same testing prompt is used in both the pre- and posttesting process.

Teachers should administer the preassessment before students begin the unit. This may be done on the day before or first day of implementation. Similarly, the postassessment should be administered when the unit has concluded. It can be administered on either the last day of implementation or closely following the last day. The suggested time frame for completing the assessment is 15 minutes.

A rubric is provided to use in scoring the instrument. Teachers should use the preassessment as a basis for judging how much students already know about leadership. The postassessment should be used to judge conceptual growth in understanding leadership.

In addition to sharing the results of the changes in learning with the students themselves, the teacher may want to aggregate the gain scores across all students. If the unit is taught over multiple years to different groups of students, the teacher will have a basis for assessing any improvements in instructional effectiveness over time. The scoring of the instrument should also lead to insights about what students absorbed or failed to absorb as a result of their experience in the classroom.

Preassessment
on the Concept of Leadership

(15 minutes)

Create a concept map to illustrate your understanding of the concept of leadership as we begin this unit of study. Draw a circle and put the word leadership in the center. Then, draw connections to that circle that describe how you understand the concept. Make as many connections as you can and label them. Then, describe the nature of the connections you have drawn.

Are there other things you know about leadership that you have not put in the concept map? Please add them below.

Name: _____ Date: _____

Postassessment
on the Concept of Leadership

Create a concept map to illustrate your understanding of the concept of leadership as we end this unit of study. Draw a circle and put the word leadership in the center. Then, draw connections to that circle that describe how you understand the concept. Make as many connections as you can and label them. Then, describe the nature of the connections you have drawn.

Are there other things you know about leadership that you have not put in the concept map? Please add them below.

Rubric for Scoring
the Pre- and Postassessments
on the Concept of Leadership

Please score each student paper according to the following dimensions of the activity. The scale goes from a 5 (*high*) to a 1 (*low*).

1. Students make appropriate *numbers* of connections to the concept.				
1 *(1–2 given)*	2 *(3–4 given)*	3 *(5–7 given)*	4 *(at least 8 examples given)*	5 *(more than 10 examples given)*

2. Students make different *types* of connections to the concept.				
1 *(only one type of connection is provided)*	2 *(two types are provided)*	3 *(three types are provided)*	4 *(four types are provided)*	5 *(five or more types are provided)*

3. Students provide an apt description of the aspect of the concept delineated or the relationship of the concept to its connection.				
1 *(only one apt description is provided)*	2 *(two apt descriptions are provided)*	3 *(three apt descriptions are provided)*	4 *(four apt descriptions are provided)*	5 *(five or more apt descriptions are provided)*

4. For additional ideas contributed about leadership, students should receive one point each, raising their score totals in uneven ways.

Add all point totals from the above items together to arrive at a student score. The top score would be 15+, depending on the fourth item on the rubric.

Part III
Lessons

Lesson 1
Introduction to the Concept of Leadership

Instructional Purpose

- ◎ To administer the Preassessment on the Concept of Leadership
- ◎ To introduce the concept of leadership
- ◎ To frame the generalizations emphasized in the unit regarding the concept of leadership
- ◎ To give students an overview of the unit and the assignments for Lessons 9 and 10

Materials Needed

- ◎ Preassessment on the Concept of Leadership
- ◎ Chart paper and wide-tipped markers
- ◎ Handout 1.1: Generalizations About Leadership
- ◎ Handout 1.2: Requirements for Leadership Biographical Study

Activities and Instructional Strategies

This lesson is constructivist in orientation, so teachers need to follow the script offered below when teaching it. This allows students to develop and articulate their own ideas about leadership before introducing the ideas emphasized in the unit.

Part I (20 minutes)

1. Administer the preassessment found in the Pre- and Postassessments and Rubric section of this unit. Do not return scoring results to students until after the postassessment has been administered at the end of the unit.

Part II (45 minutes)

1. Organize students into groups of 4–5 to complete the following activities:
   - ○ Ask students to name as many people as they can who are leaders and to write the leader's name and his or her role or area of expertise on the chart paper. Specify that they need to come up with 30 examples that encompass the United States and other countries within 5 minutes. After 2 minutes, prompt students to think locally and regionally as well as nationally and internationally. After 5 minutes, call time.

○ Have each group share its list. Create a master list using just the last name of examples cited by the first group and then continue adding new examples that each subsequent group shares. Prompt the second and subsequent groups to not repeat any names cited by the prior groups. (This requires that they listen to what the other groups are sharing.)

○ Have each group categorize the domains in which its list of leaders have contributed. After 3 minutes, prompt them to offer up alternative ways of categorizing the examples of leaders other than by domain. Call time after 5 minutes.

○ Ask each group to share its domain categories. Create a master list of the domains of leadership generated. Ask students why some categories have several leaders but others have so few. Ask students what other schematic they proposed as a way to categorize their lists of leaders.

○ Return to the small-group format and have each group list nonexamples (people who are not exemplary of leadership qualities). Allow students to grapple with this instruction without offering clarification.

○ Ask groups to share their nonexamples and construct a master list. Ask the whole group: What qualities or traits, if any, do these people have in common? What qualities keep them from becoming leaders?

○ Return to the small-group format and have each group generate 2–3 generalizations about leadership. Tell them that a generalization is a statement that is always or almost always true. The generalizations should be derived by distinguishing the group of people identified as leaders from the group identified as nonleaders. The generalizations should cut across all domains.

○ Ask each group to share only one generalization and to pick one that has not yet been shared. Add each of these generalizations to the master chart that has been created by the whole class. If time allows, probe whether each generalization truly distinguishes between the leaders and the nonleaders.

2. If time is running short, groups can share their generalizations during the next class period as long as the student work has been saved (chart paper with generalizations for each group).

3. Assign the homework for Lesson 2 at this point in the process (see the Homework section). Students will need more than one night to complete the Internet research required for each leader studied.

1. Reorient the class to the list of generalizations created by students in the previous period. Distribute Handout 1.1: Generalizations About Leadership and have students compare the two lists using the following questions as prompts:
   o Where do you see overlap in the two lists?
   o What ideas did your group consider that are not reflected on Handout 1.1 and vice versa?
   o Are there any generalizations that do not fit the work done so far? Explain.
   o Can you think of another important generalization that is not reflected on either of the two lists?
   o Which student-generated generalization would the group most like to add to the list being studied in this unit?

2. Have students add a ninth generalization selected by consensus to Handout 1.1 to incorporate the generalization they have selected as a group.
3. Ask students to choose one generalization from the list of nine and write three arguments or justifications explaining why leaders need to possess or address the attribute or behavior embedded in or associated with the generalization. (Allow 15 minutes for the writing activity.)
4. Ask students to share 3–5 examples orally. Distribute file folders or binders. Have students begin a portfolio of their writing for use during the unit and include this piece as their first entry.

Part IV (15 minutes)

1. Give students a brief overview of the unit. Explain that they will be studying the concept of leadership by examining the lives of selected leaders—both contemporary and historical—as well as some of the research literature from various fields such as business, education, and social science. Identify the six individuals being studied by the whole class (Oprah Winfrey, Steve Jobs, Dwight D. Eisenhower, Thurgood Marshall, Maya Lin, and Nikola Tesla).
2. Brief students on the requirements for the final class project, which is an oral presentation and written report on an autobiography or biography of a leader. As they prepare and deliver their oral presentations, they should think of themselves as leaders in motivating their classmates to share their interests in their selected leader and to value that person's contributions to society. Distribute Handout 1.2: Requirements for Leadership

Biographical Study detailing the requirements for this project. The presentation and written report criteria outlined on Handout 1.2 will be evaluated by the teacher in Lesson 10 (see Teacher Template 10.1: Evaluation Form for Student Presentation and Teacher Template 10.2: Evaluation Form for Written Report). Answer any questions students have.

Part V (15 minutes or less)

1. Tell students that in one of the future class periods, there will be a local panel of leaders visiting the class to discuss the concept of leadership. Announce a date for this panel. Ask students whom they would like to invite to speak on this panel. Prioritize the names on the list and limit the panel size to four. Assign individual students responsibility for inviting each of the candidates. Set a time frame so that if a candidate declines the invitation, the next person on the list can be contacted. Have students report back to you within one week as to whether or not the panel member is willing and available to participate. In some cases, it might be more appropriate for the teacher to contact the proposed panel members.
2. As an alternative, the teacher may determine the composition of and make the contacts for the panel him- or herself. There is a greater likelihood of success if this can be done earlier rather than later in the planning process.
3. Tell students that about midway through the unit they will be developing questions to ask the panel, so as subsequent lessons unfold, they should keep this in mind.

Assessment

Teachers should use the constructed work of students as the basis for judging their initial understanding of the concept of leadership. Insert the student writing on arguments/justifications into the portfolios. Be sure to collect the preassessment. You may return the pre- and postassessments after the end of the unit.

Homework

The first biographical research should be assigned as homework. They should be given a copy of Handout 2.1: Biographical Chart: Oprah Winfrey, found in the next lesson, to help guide their reading and to use for taking notes. Students should be instructed to fill out each element in the Biographical Chart with at least five pieces of information that have been culled from their reading. Students must read all four of the biographical entries on the following Internet sites in their entirety and select the data that they want to highlight in their charts:

- Wikipedia (http://en.wikipedia.org/wiki/Oprah_Winfrey)
- Academy of Achievement (http://www.achievement.org/autodoc/page/win0bio-1)
- IMDb Biography (http://www.imdb.com/name/nm0001856/bio)
- Biography from Answers.com (http://www.answers.com/topic/oprah-winfrey)

Extensions

There are no extensions for this lesson.

Handout 1.1
Generalizations About Leadership

◎ Leadership requires vision—the ability to see beyond what is to what might be by bridging the present and the future.

◎ Leadership requires the ability to influence and motivate others to work in concert to achieve the vision.

◎ Leadership recognizes the inevitability of conflict and uses it to clarify purpose, galvanize commitment, and support personal growth.

◎ Leadership in a given field fosters creativity and innovation in that field.

◎ Leadership is judged through the lens of time and history.

◎ Leadership is highly dependent on the interplay of intellectual abilities, specific aptitudes and skills, and personality factors.

◎ Leadership requires strong beliefs and core values and the passion and tenacity to act in accordance with them.

◎ Leadership is grounded in knowledge of self and the belief in human agency to change the world.

Handout 1.2

Requirements for Leadership Biographical Study

1. Select an individual whose biography or autobiography you would like to read. The book must be at an adult reading level, not one designed for middle school students or younger. The teacher must preapprove selections in advance of undertaking the reading. Submit in writing your book title and author by _____ to secure approval.

2. You must prepare a written report on your chosen leader and make a 5–7 minute oral presentation to your classmates. The report and presentation must address the following components:

   o Introduce the leader and explain what his or her claim to fame is. Give a little background and history on the person by selecting 10 interesting points about his or her life that are drawn from the categories in the biographical charts used in this unit to study leaders (e.g., early family background and created family structure, major career/professional events and accomplishments, personal life themes/ beliefs, selected quotations).

   o Describe in your own words what you think this person's lasting impact and contributions are to the field or domain in which he or she operates.

   o Explain the most important thing you learned about the concept of leadership by reading about the life of this person and identify any new insights that you uncovered as a result of your work that extended, amplified, revised, or contradicted your understanding of the concept of leadership.

   o Make a brief analytical assessment of the quality of the book you read and state your reasons for this assessment. In other words, would you recommend this book to other students? Why or why not?

3. You may use visual, audio, and/or other electronic aids in making your oral presentation.

4. Use both the written and oral reports as opportunities to showcase some of the ideas we have studied in this unit about communicating effectively and motivating others.

Presentation Criteria

The presentation:
◎ is thoughtful and well organized,
◎ demonstrates deep knowledge of the biographical subject,
◎ incorporates formatting effectively,
◎ is creative, and
◎ engages the audience.

Written Report Criteria

The written report:
◎ is clear and well organized,
◎ is comprehensive in addressing the required components,
◎ integrates ideas about the leader with conceptions of leadership studied in the unit,
◎ offers insights about the leader's life with respect to his or her work and legacy, and
◎ is mechanically competent with respect to grammar, usage, and spelling.

Lesson 2
Oprah Winfrey and Vision

Passion is energy. Feel the power that comes from focusing on what excites you.

—Oprah Winfrey

Instructional Purpose

◎ To introduce the use of the Internet to do biographical research
◎ To map biographical data against key leadership factors
◎ To examine and apply ideas that relate to the concept of vision in leadership

Materials Needed

◎ Handout 2.1: Biographical Chart: Oprah Winfrey
◎ Handout 2.2: List of Universal Fears and Needs
◎ Handout 2.3: Prospectus for SHINE (Students Help Inspire Network Excellence)
◎ Handout 2.4: Journal Entry Questions
◎ Teachers' Rap Sheet on Oprah Winfrey (see Appendix A)

Activities and Instructional Strategies

Part I (1 period if homework was completed)

1. In the homework assignment for the previous lesson, students were directed to use the Internet to collect biographical data on Oprah Winfrey, media mogul, television personality, award-winning actress, and philanthropist. Students were required to read the biographical information on all of the sites even though there is overlap among them. Once the class has been convened as a whole group, ask students how old Oprah is today. This will orient them to her status as a contemporary leader.

2. Because this is the first lesson involving student research using Internet sites, the teacher may prefer to use in-class time to have students conduct the biographical research. The teacher may allocate time at the beginning of the class for students to examine the recommended sites and identify and select three critical elements to showcase for each section of Handout 2.1: Biographical Chart: Oprah Winfrey. Refer to the Homework section of the previous lesson to find the website references to give to the stu-

dents. If this is done at the beginning of class, allow an additional period for the completion of the whole lesson.

3. Another option for implementing this component of the lesson is to assign individual students, dyads, or small groups only a portion of the elements in the chart. For instance, the elements on early family background and created family structure, education, personality characteristics and areas of aptitude, talent, and interest, major career/professional events and accomplishments, and personal life themes/beliefs could be assigned to one group. Other elements would then be assigned to different groups. All of the students would be expected to read all of the material, but they would only have to document the data for the elements that they or their groups have been assigned.

4. Have the whole class complete a master Biographical Chart on Oprah Winfrey by using a white board or overhead projector to compile the information gathered by students. The teacher should start by asking: What did you discover about Ms. Winfrey's early family background and created family structure? What did you discover about her education? Follow this format until the master chart has been completed enough to ensure that the students have a fairly in-depth profile of the individual. The teacher may choose to annotate or extend the information in the Biographical Chart by drawing on the data provided in the Teachers' Rap Sheet found in Appendix A. Students should embellish their own charts as the class session unfolds.

5. Conclude the lesson by telling students that the class will be following a similar pattern for all of the biographies studied. Sometimes the aggregation of data will be done in small groups, rather than by the whole class. Use this time to make any adjustments in the instructions to students about what they are to look for in reading the background material or in completing their Biographical Charts. At this point in this lesson and in subsequent lessons, you may want to share the next homework assignment so that students have several days to complete their individual biographical research for the next leader to be studied.

Part II (1 period)

1. The teacher will engage students in a large-group discussion using the following questions:
   o In what ways is Oprah Winfrey a leader? (Probe for justification if needed.)
   o To what extent did time, place, and circumstances impact her ability to become a leader?

o How would you describe the vision that Oprah Winfrey has brought to the field of multimedia (film, television, theater, magazines)? How would you describe her vision for network television in her role as co-owner of OWN (Oprah Winfrey Network)?

o What evidence is there of initiative, perseverance, and risk taking in Ms. Winfrey's profile?

o What other personal characteristics contributed to Oprah Winfrey's phenomenal success as a talk show hostess? Were the characteristics that underscored her abilities to launch a monthly magazine and to acquire a television network the same or different? In what ways has she grown or changed over the course of her career to date?

o What do you see as Ms. Winfrey's lasting impact and contributions in the entertainment industry based on what you know at this time? What innovations and/or improvements can you credit her with pioneering in her field? How would you describe her contributions beyond this field as they impacted racial and gender relationships, educational initiatives, and her agenda of personal change and empowerment?

o Ms. Winfrey said: "My philosophy is that not only are you responsible for your life, but doing the best at this moment puts you in the best place for the next moment." How would you paraphrase this statement? What values can be inferred from this statement?

o Ask: If you were to create a rock opera based on the life of Ms. Winfrey, what would be the title or tagline for the theme song? For the musically inclined student, ask him or her to hum or sing a few bars. (Allow students a few minutes to compose their answers to this question.)

Part III (1+ period)

1. Tell the class that this component of the lesson focuses on the concept of vision in leadership (the first generalization). Ask for a definition of vision in this context (e.g., a mental picture of a future state, situation, or outcome that galvanizes others to action) and as the definition evolves, probe for adjectives or phrases that describe vision (e.g., a little cloudy but grand, evocative of feelings as well as intellect, crystallizes the future, meaningful, worthy of achievement, taps into common needs, starting point). Write student responses on the board as they emerge from dialogue. Then, tell the class that you are going to provide some information on an additional consideration in examining the concept of vision that will help them think about this process more deeply.

2. Distribute Handout 2.2: List of Universal Fears and Needs and present a mini-lecture on its content using the following information.

○ In his book entitled *The One Thing You Need to Know About Great Managing, Great Leading, and Sustained Individual Success*, Marcus Buckingham (2005) made the point that managing and leading are different propositions and that one of the behaviors that distinguishes between the two is the focus on uniqueness versus universality. Managers need to discover what is unique about each person (talents, skills, knowledge, and/or experiences) and then capitalize on this uniqueness to help each member of the team maximize his or her contributions and potential for success. Leaders recognize that each person is different, but often choose to focus instead on what is shared among us. They are not intermediaries capable of linking the individuals' talents with the tasks they are assigned to do; they are instigators whose role is to rally people toward a better future.

○ One way to think about what is universal is to draw on the work of anthropologist Donald Brown, who investigated and compiled a list of human universals drawn from multiple cultures across the world. Buckingham distilled this list to a pairing of five fears and their five corresponding needs that he believed leaders should focus on. Although all five have some relevance to the art of leading, one should command the greatest attention.

- *Fear of Death (our own and our family's)—The Need for Security.* Because every society fears death, celebrates fertility, and prohibits murder and suicide, we have a strong need to secure our own lives and those of our loved ones.

- *Fear of the Outsider—The Need for Community.* People fear strangers and make rules to define membership for the group. We organize ourselves to keep the herd strong. Community gives us a degree of safety, identity, and acceptance, and expands our comfort zone.

- *Fear of Chaos—The Need for Authority and Order.* Every society has a creation myth that begins with overriding chaos, and every society establishes systems of classification in order to organize their world. From this desire springs a need for authority, for someone or some collective to take charge. Laws, structures, and systems evolve to stabilize the community and regulate acceptable behavior.

- *Fear of Insignificance—The Need for Respect.* Although the distribution of power among individuals varies within each society, all societies see the individual as having worth distinct from the group. Each society has a word for self-image and belief that a positive self-image is better than a negative one, which underscores the craving for prestige and the respect that comes with it.

- *Fear of the Future—The Need for Clarity*. Every society has a concept of the future and a word for hope. Because the future is instable, unknown, and potentially dangerous, it engenders a level of fear. Prestige is given to those who claim to be able to predict the future whether they are seers or shamans or stockbrokers or politicians.

3. Ask students which of these dualities is of most utility to potential leaders. If they ask, tell them that Buckingham identifies the last as the most important. Buckingham goes on to state that the most effective way to turn fear into confidence is to be clear: to define the future in such vivid terms that others can see where you are headed.

4. Conclude the mini-lecture by asking students if they have any questions about the concept of vision. Ask if they can think of anyone who is or has been a great leader who does not appear to have had a sense of vision for what needed to be addressed or accomplished.

5. Distribute Handout 2.3: Prospectus for SHINE (Students Help Inspire Network Excellence) and tell students they can consider some of the ideas just presented as they work together on the next activity in this part of the lesson.

6. Break students into small groups and tell them their task is to create a prospectus for a new television show for OWN. It is 2012, and they are stepping in to help Oprah Winfrey develop program ideas that will increase viewership and ultimately the revenues needed to turn her enterprise into a success. Their assignment is to come up with an idea for a new TV program that aligns with the vision and values of the network, to provide enough details so that the idea can be evaluated by network executives, and to present and market the idea so that it is accepted rather than rejected by the network's brass.

7. Reconvene the whole class and have each group present the ideas in its prospectus. Have the class vote on which of the ideas has the most likelihood of being accepted by the network executives. Ask them whether the idea that is voted the most likely to succeed is also the idea that would be the most educational. If it is not obvious, ask them how they incorporated the Buckingham observation about uniqueness versus universality into their thinking as they explored potential ideas for the new show or for marketing the new show.

Part IV (1 period or less)

1. Distribute Handout 2.4: Journal Entry Questions to students and allow them 15–20 minutes to select at least two and complete their journal

entries. As an option, the teacher may assign specific questions to individuals or to the whole class.

2. After the time has elapsed, ask for some volunteers to share their responses and discuss the questions as a whole class.

3. This part may also be done as homework as long as it will not interfere with the completion of the biographical research on the next leader.

Assessment

The teacher should check to see that each student has completed two written pieces for the implementation of the lesson: Handout 2.1 (unless assigned as a group project) and the journal entry. In addition, the teacher should collect copies of Handout 2.3 completed by the groups and should make sufficient copies so that each group member can have a copy of the group's response for his or her own portfolio. At the top of each original form, write "group work" before making the copies.

Homework

Students are assigned responsibility for completing Handout 3.1: Biographical Chart: Steve Jobs in preparation for the next class period. The four sites that students should be directed to for conducting this research are as follows:

- Wikipedia (http://en.wikipedia.org/wiki/Steve_Jobs)
- Timeline (http://allaboutstevejobs.com/bio/timeline.php)
- Biography from Answers.com (http://www.answers.com/topic/steve-jobs)
- theGrio (http://thegrio.com/2011/10/05/apple-company-co-founder-steve-jobs-has-died/)

Extensions

The following ideas are offered as substitutions for parts of the above lesson or as extensions for this lesson focusing on Oprah Winfrey and the concept of vision in leadership.

- Have students view the video clip of the speech given by Oprah Winfrey to the graduating class at Stanford University on June 15, 2008 on YouTube. Have them write a critique that responds to the following probes:
  - What are the three main points that Oprah shares in her speech?
  - What values emerge from the lessons she shares and the stories she highlights in the speech that give you a sense of her personal integrity and/or leadership stature?
  - What elements or techniques does she employ to secure the attention of her audience and how effective are these?

◎ Have students read Neil Baldwin's introduction of Oprah Winfrey (http://www.nationalbook.org/nbaacceptspeech_owinfrey_intro. html#.UFOcX0JwYc4) and Winfrey's acceptance speech (http://www. nationalbook.org/nbaacceptspeech_owinfrey.html#.UFOccUJwYc4) for the 50th Anniversary Gold Medal Award of the National Book Foundation delivered in 1999. Have them write a paragraph or two about what they learned about Ms. Winfrey from this reading selection that amplifies their understanding of her leadership skills and abilities. She references four authors in this speech (Maya Angelou, Wally Lamb, Toni Morrison, and Alice Walker); have students investigate the contributions of at least two of these writers and speculate as to why they resonated so strongly with Ms. Winfrey. In tandem with this part, have students identify an author whose work speaks to them and comment on why they think they have connected with that particular author or work in terms of their own interests and values.

◎ Perhaps the most predominant theme in Oprah Winfrey's life has been her message of empowerment of the self. In *Talent Is Never Enough Workbook*, John C. Maxwell (2007) identifies 13 key choices that can be made to maximize a person's talent. The first of these is that belief lifts your talent. He noted, "The first and greatest obstacle to success for most people is their belief in themselves" (p. 1). Have students create a profile sheet about their prevailing beliefs about themselves by answering the following questions:

  o What are your beliefs about yourself?

  o How do these beliefs affect your behavior?

  o What self-imposed limitations or shortcomings do you place on yourself and from where did these ideas spring?

  o What type of person do you have the potential to become?

  o What truth about your potential can you use to replace any of your limiting beliefs?

  o To what end would you direct your energies if you were to realize your full potential?

  o How can this vision of yourself and your mission energize you to move forward?

◎ Have students examine the website for the Oprah Winfrey Leadership Academy for Girls (http://owla.co.za). Ask them to draw inferences about the vision that Oprah was able to turn into a reality in terms of the design and execution of this state-of-the-art secondary school for girls. Then have students draft an expository essay on this vision, on what the design of the school reveals about the teaching of leadership skills, on what the expectations for success are, and on what is learned about Oprah from a close-up look at this philanthropic achievement. If necessary, offer some prompts to stimulate students' reflections on this matter:

- Why did Oprah start this academy?
- What statements has she made that help to explain her vision for the academy?
- Why did she choose South Africa for its location?
- What in her background and experience make this a logical or illogical choice for a major philanthropic undertaking?
- What do you think made her successful in tackling an initiative outside her sphere of expertise?
- What specific values are reflected in the admission and graduation policies and requirements?
- What did you learn about the breadth and scope of Oprah's leadership abilities from your examination of the Leadership Academy?

Handout 2.1
Biographical Chart: Oprah Winfrey

Full Name: _____

Lifespan: _____

Early Family Background and Created Family Structure

_____

_____

_____

Personality Characteristics and Areas of Aptitude, Talent, and Interest

_____

_____

_____

Major Career/Professional Events and Accomplishments

_____

_____

_____

Personal Life Themes/Beliefs

_____

_____

_____

Selected Quotations

_____

_____

_____

Awards and Recognition

_____

_____

_____

_____

Handout 2.2

List of Universal Fears and Needs

(as categorized by Marcus Buckingham)

◎ Fear of Death (our own and our family's)—The Need for Security

◎ Fear of the Outsider—The Need for Community

◎ Fear of Chaos—The Need for Authority and Order

◎ Fear of Insignificance—The Need for Respect

◎ Fear of the Future—The Need for Clarity

Prospectus for SHINE

(Students Help Inspire Network Excellence)

Oprah Winfrey Network (OWN) Background

Vision for OWN

OWN is about the "notion of self-discovery" told through "moments of personal transformation" and focused on the message of empowerment. "It is intended to inspire and entertain people around issues of money, weight, health, relationships, spirit, helping people to raise their children and giving back." Its focus is to teach people to be all that they can be without becoming "treacly" or "preachy" (Levin, 2009, para. 3–5).

Ownership of OWN

OWN is an American specialty channel produced by Harpo Productions (Winfrey) and Discovery Communications that debuted January 1, 2011 in approximately 80 million homes.

Composition of Programs

OWN is designed to offer a mix of original programs, specialty programs, original documentaries, and acquired movies. Its targeted demographic is 25–54-year-old women.

Status as of April 2012

On March 22, 2012, Louisa Ada Seltzer reported that OWN was expected to lose $142.9 million dollars in its first year of operation. Earlier, the network had laid off one fifth of its staff, primarily due to low ratings. As of March 2012, the network averaged 180,000 viewers a day (Serjeant, 2012). Ms. Winfrey acknowledged in an interview on *CBS This Morning* that network ownership was much harder than she anticipated and that she regretted launching it before she felt that everything had been put into place to make it successful.

Prospectus Instructions

Please provide the following information for SHINE on the attached form:
- ◎ A brief description of your idea (vision) for a program that will improve the fortunes of OWN.
- ◎ The target audience for the program and in what time slot it will air.
- ◎ Specification of any special parameters, such as star power needed, extraordinary cost factors incurred, liability concerns, and accessibility of location for shooting.

◎ An explanation for how your idea (vision) supports and/or complements the network's overarching vision.

◎ A rationale for why your idea will be successful and an estimate of the number of new viewers who will be drawn in (metric for success).

References

Levin, G. (2009, December 2). Here's what to expect on Oprah's OWN cable network. *USA Today*. Retrieved from http://www.usatoday.com/life/television/news/2009-12-02-own02_ST_N.htm

Seltzer, L. A. (2012, March 22). Report: OWN will lose $142.9 million this year. *Media Life*. Retrieved from http://www.medialifemagazine.com:8080/artman2/publish/Hereandthere/Report-OWN-will-lose-142-9-million-this-year.asp

Serjeant, J. (2012). *OWN viewers up as Oprah's added presence pays off.* Retrieved from http://www.reuters.com/article/2012/03/28/us-oprah-own-idUSBRE82R1JH20120328

Prospectus Form for SHINE

Brief description of your idea (vision):

Target audience and time slot:

Special parameters (if any):

Linkage to network's vision statement:

Rationale for expected success and estimate of new viewership (metric for success):

Handout 2.4
Journal Entry Questions

1. What did you learn from the biographical study of Oprah Winfrey that is particularly illuminating in your understanding of leadership? In what ways is Oprah Winfrey a role model for you and other emerging leaders?

2. Is there a relationship between celebrity and leadership? Describe points of intersection and divergence as you see them. Which is most valued in our culture and why?

3. What do you see as the strengths and shortcomings of using the Internet for biographical research? Did you uncover any mistakes or misinformation in gathering data on Ms. Winfrey? If so, what were they, and how did you discover them? Where would you go next if you wanted to learn about Ms. Winfrey's life in more depth?

4. Much of the research base on the topic of leadership stresses the criticality of vision for leadership effectiveness. What did you learn about the concept of vision that you may not have understood or considered before? How do you think one develops one's capacity for vision?

Lesson 3
Steve Jobs and Storytelling

A lot of people in our industry haven't had very diverse experiences. So they don't have enough dots to connect, and they end up with very linear solutions without a broad perspective on the problem. The broader one's understanding of the human experience, the better design we will have.

—Steve Jobs

Instructional Purpose

- ◎ To practice using the Internet to do biographical research
- ◎ To map biographical data against key leadership factors
- ◎ To explore and apply the use of storytelling to motivate others

Materials Needed

- ◎ Teacher's Answer Key for Handout 3.3: Key Points and Storytelling Critique of Steve Jobs's Speech
- ◎ Handout 3.1: Biographical Chart: Steve Jobs
- ◎ Handout 3.2: Leadership Storytelling Checklist
- ◎ Handout 3.3: Key Points and Storytelling Critique of Steve Jobs's Speech
- ◎ Handout 3.4: Journal Entry Questions
- ◎ Teachers' Rap Sheet on Steve Jobs (see Appendix A)

Activities and Instructional Strategies

Part I (1 period)

1. In the homework assignment for the previous lesson, students were directed to the Internet to collect biographical data on Steve Jobs, cofounder and former chairman and CEO of Apple, Inc. and a visionary and pioneer in the field of computer-related technology. (Note that one of the websites contains a 15-minute video clip of Jobs's commencement address at Stanford. This will be reshown to the whole class during Part III of the lesson. It is intentional that students watch it twice.) Students are expected to have read all of the material and viewed the video clip. To start the lesson, ask students how old Steve Jobs would be if he were alive today. This will orient them to his status as a contemporary leader. For alternatives to doing the research as homework or for doing only portions of the Biographical Chart, see Part I of Lesson 2.

2. Group students into groups of 4–5 and have them create master charts on Steve Jobs using the information collected by each student. As they review their charts, advise them to add any important points that have not been recorded but that they remember from reading the material. After allowing 30–35 minutes for this, ask the groups some questions that will ensure that they have retrieved some of the most salient information about Mr. Jobs. Sample questions are as follows:

   o What evidence did you find that Mr. Jobs was precocious as a youngster? At what age was he first exposed to a computer?
   o What were some of his positive and negative personality characteristics?
   o Who did he partner with to design the first "blue boxes"? What precipitated his return to Apple in 1996 after having been fired from the company he started?
   o What would you say were the three biggest achievements of his career?
   o In 2009, what did teenagers select Jobs as? Why do you think he was picked that year?

3. The teacher may choose to annotate the information collected by drawing on the Teachers' Rap Sheet for Steve Jobs if students have failed to grasp and/or record important pieces of biographical information.

4. Conclude this part of the lesson by pointing out that both Jobs and Winfrey were entrepreneurs. Ask students who was more of a visionary: Oprah Winfrey or Steve Jobs? If time allows, have them pick one and write a paragraph or two justifying their choice for inclusion in their portfolios.

Part II (1 period)

1. The teacher will engage students in a large-group discussion using the following questions:

   o In what ways was Steve Jobs a leader? (Probe for justification if needed.) Both Jobs and Winfrey are leaders in business—one in the media/entertainment business and the other in the technology business. How is leadership similar across these foci, and how is it different?
   o To what extent did time, place, and circumstances impact Steve's ability to become a leader?
   o How would you describe the vision that Steve brought to the field of computer technology? How did this vision evolve from his early days in building a desktop computer for personal use to the creation of the iPad?
   o What evidence is there of initiative, perseverance, and risk taking in Mr. Jobs's profile?

- ○ What other personal characteristics contributed to Steve Jobs's phenomenal success as a technology guru and entrepreneur? In what ways, if any, did Mr. Jobs evidence personal growth or change over the course of his life?
- ○ What do you see as Mr. Jobs's lasting impact and contributions in the field of technology? What innovations and/or improvements can you credit him with pioneering in this field? Were these innovations linear or exponential? What contributions to society did he make beyond his field of expertise?
- ○ Mr. Jobs said:

  > I'm an optimist in the sense that I believe humans are noble and honorable, and some of them are really smart. I have a very optimistic view of individuals. . . . I have a somewhat more pessimistic view of people in groups.

  How would you paraphrase this statement? Why would he make this distinction? How would this belief impact his role as a leader and/ or his leadership style?
- ○ What would you write if you were asked to create a six-word biography for Steve Jobs? Ask for volunteers to share their ideas. (Allow students a few minutes to think about their answers to this question.)

Part III (1+ period)

1. Tell the class that this component of the lesson focuses on the role of motivating and influencing others in leadership (the second generalization). Ask the class if anyone remembers how Jobs introduced his commencement address at Stanford. ("I want to tell you three stories from my life.")
2. Present a mini-lecture on storytelling in leadership using the following information.
   - ○ Much attention has been paid in contemporary leadership literature to the importance of storytelling as a critical communication skill for leadership success. Robert Mai and Alan Akerson, in *The Leader as Communicator* (2003), underscored the value of storytelling as a motivational technique for leveraging attention and shaping perspective and commitment. They wrote:

     > Who doesn't like to hear a good story? Stories are the way we think, remember, communicate; the way we create

meaning, coherence, and trust. Story-telling is pervasive in our lives. . . . We make decisions based on how well stories hang together, their narrative logic. When we listen to a new story line, we compare it to other narratives we already know. . . . we decide if the new story, or some combination of new and old, is better able to describe the reality of our [own situation or experience]. (Mai & Akerson, 2003, p. 61)

○ According to Mai and Akerson (2003), a story performs valuable functions in the exercise of leadership:
- It arranges information into a logical sequence.
- It can give meaning to experiences that lack meaning in themselves.
- It can illuminate an underlying theme or pattern that has gone unnoticed.
- It can provide a rationale for decisions made.
- It can bring closure or synthesis to a situation or series of situations.
- It can add emotional undertones and overtones to a dry and factual landscape.
- It can elevate the level of interest of the recipient or audience hearing the story.
- It can set actions or events in a moral context.

○ Kouzes and Posner (1999) emphasized storytelling as a way to teach virtues during critical incidents and to celebrate the contributions of individuals and groups in achieving the mission or in making progress toward this end. These authors also cited some tips from Gail Wilson on how to improve storytelling abilities (p. 240):
- Use real-life examples.
- Keep a small notebook or diary to record ideas and experiences.
- Give stories interesting titles.
- Talk about what you know.

○ For stories to be effective, they need to be clear, comprehensive, and compelling (Mai & Akerson, 2003). Clear means simple, direct, and told in plain language. Comprehensive means that things aren't left out, the pieces are connected, and the listener finds a point of connection to the story. Compelling means that the listener desires to hear the whole story from the beginning to the end and that the story captures or "nails" the idea or point that is being made. A variety of narrative techniques can be used to make stories compelling, such as making them action-oriented, casting people who are known into the roles in the story, using the past as prologue to a new story, and portraying the current situation as the beginning or middle of a shared journey.

3. Distribute Handout 3.2: Leadership Storytelling Checklist and go over the items with students.

4. Conclude the mini-lecture by asking students if they have any questions about the use of storytelling in communicating ideas and information in the exercise of leadership. Can they think of anyone who is a great leader who is particularly well known for his or her ability to tell stories for such purposes? Let them come up with two or three examples.

5. Show the video clip of Jobs's commencement address at Stanford (from 2005) to the whole class. (This will be the second viewing for students, but it will focus their attention on the structure and content of the speech.) Before running the clip, distribute Handout 3.3: Key Points and Storytelling Critique of Steve Jobs's Speech to use in recording their assessments. Tell students their assignment is twofold. First, they should identify the three main ideas that Jobs has embedded in his stories. Second, they should critique the effectiveness of each of the three stories in meeting the criteria on the checklist. After students have completed their review of the speech, debrief the assignment by asking what the three main ideas were (tweaking the responses to ensure that they are reasonably accurate) and overall how well Jobs did in meeting the criteria established. (See Teacher's Answer Key for Handout 3.3: Key Points and Storytelling Critique of Steve Jobs's Speech for the three main ideas.)

6. Tell students that in the next class session they will be given time to prepare a personal story to share. The purpose of the story will be to make a point that will impact others' knowledge, understanding, behavior, or values. This will give students an opportunity to be thinking about their own stories and how they can be shaped to influence their peers beforehand.

Part IV (1 period)

1. The teacher will give students 15–20 minutes to prepare to tell a 4–5-minute story about an event or experience in their lives (it may be about themselves or a close relative for whom the event/experience impacted the student in some way) that can be used to make a point. Remind students that storytelling in leadership is often used to help people see the bigger picture (vision), to give deeper meaning or understanding to situations, to provide a way of organizing information into

a cohesive whole, to bring closure to a situation, and to celebrate milestones, accomplishments, and contributions.

2. If students have trouble grasping this assignment, have them create a scenario for the use of the story. For instance, imagine that their story is being used to (a) encourage one of the school's teams to overcome early season losses, (b) build trust in one's peers in pursuit of a bid for student council or class president, (c) address or correct problem behavior observed (bullying, cheating), or (d) illuminate the deeper meaning of school rites such as induction into honor societies or school graduation ceremonies.

3. Have students tell their stories to the class. After each oration, make a comment that compliments the speaker on at least two aspects of the presentation. Ask each student what aspect he or she feels could have been strengthened. If the technology is available, video each speech and make copies for students to include in their portfolios.

Part V (1 period or less)

1. Distribute Handout 3.4: Journal Entry Questions to students and allow them 15–20 minutes to select at least two and complete their journal entries. As an option, you may assign specific questions to individuals or to the whole class.

2. After the time has elapsed, ask for some volunteers to share their responses and discuss the questions as a whole class.

3. This part may also be done as homework as long as there is sufficient time between this class and the next one for the biographical research on the next leader to be completed.

Assessment

The teacher should check to see that each student has completed three written pieces for the implementation of the lesson: Handout 3.1 (unless assigned as a group project), Handout 3.3, and the journal entry. In addition, the teacher should have students insert their notes or text for their speeches (or video clip, if made available to them) into their portfolios.

Homework

Students are assigned responsibility for completing Handout 4.1: Biographical Chart: Dwight D. Eisenhower in preparation for the next class period. The five sites that students should be directed to for conducting this research are as follows:

◎ Eisenhower Foundation (http://www.dwightdeisenhower.com/whats
new.html)
◎ Miller Center (http://millercenter.org/president/eisenhower)
◎ Wikipedia (http://en.wikipedia.org/wiki/Dwight_D._Eisenhower)
◎ Biography.com (http://www.biography.com/people/dwight-d-
eisenhower-9285482)
◎ BrainyQuote (http://www.brainyquote.com/quotes/authors/d/dwight_
d_eisenhower.html)

This will be the first biography of a leader who is not a contemporary of the
students. To this end, the teacher may want to present a context for the period
of time that President Eisenhower served. This can be done when assigning the
homework or when introducing Part I of Lesson 4. Highlight a few of the fol-
lowing events that might be of interest to your students that occurred during the
Eisenhower administration:
◎ The 1954 Supreme Court decision on *Brown v. Board of Education* (end
of segregated schools)
◎ The invention of the Salk vaccine to combat polio
◎ The rise of McCarthyism
◎ The division of Vietnam into north and south
◎ The establishment of the Warsaw Pact, which escalated tensions in
Europe
◎ The rise in use of TVs and cars, as well as the introduction of fast food
restaurants
◎ The opening of Disneyland in California
◎ The 1959 overthrow of the Batista regime by Fidel Castro in Cuba

Extensions

The following ideas are offered as substitutions for parts of the above lesson
or as extensions for this lesson focusing on Steve Jobs and the use of storytelling
in leadership.
◎ Have students compare, contrast, and do an evaluative assessment of the
video clips of the speech given by Oprah Winfrey to the graduating class
at Stanford University on June 15, 2008 and the speech given by Steve
Jobs on June 12, 2005.
◎ Storytelling in literature is used to entertain and uplift; in history, it is
used to make the past come alive; and in counseling, it is used for self-
awareness and self-reflection. In leadership, stories may be used for
multiple purposes, but they are often recommended as a motivational
strategy to influence team members or followers. Have students identify

a story from their own experience and tell it for at least three different purposes. Ask them to think about what elements they change, amplify, delete, diminish, or exaggerate in the story as it is designed to serve different ends or to reach different audiences. Have students explain the differences to ensure that they are cognizant of the reasons for the choices they have made. They may do this as a written exercise or an oral exercise by audio- or videotaping the assignment.

◎ For students interested in technology, share the 96-minute interview of Steve Jobs by Walter Mossberg (technology columnist for the *Wall Street Journal*) conducted at the G8 Conference in 2010 available on YouTube. (Note: There is some profanity used in the interview by Mr. Jobs. Please use your discretion on whether or not this is appropriate for your students.) Have students write responses to some or all of the following questions:

   o What did you learn about how Mr. Jobs approaches problem solving and making mistakes at Apple?
   o What did you observe about how he handles intrusive or prying questions?
   o What observations can you make about his business philosophy, how business decisions are made, and the core values at Apple?
   o There is probably no other industry that is as vulnerable to rapid change as the technology industry. What did you learn about how Mr. Jobs understands the concept of change and about how he manages it?
   o What did you learn about how Apple is organized and the role of teamwork in the organization?
   o When Mr. Jobs alluded to the line "Isn't it funny . . . a ship that leaks from the top . . .," what did he mean?
   o In what ways did this interview impact your understanding of Mr. Jobs's leadership skills?

◎ Have students watch the documentary, *iGenius: How Steve Jobs Changed the World*, which can be found online at Vimeo, for a 43-minute overview of Jobs's impact on the field of technology and a tribute to his genius. After viewing, have students critique the film from the standpoint of storytelling by answering these questions:

   o How effectively does the documentary tell the story of Jobs's contributions to the field of technology?
   o What techniques does the medium of film use to capture and hold the viewer's interest?

- What is the main point the creators of the film want the viewer to take away from the film?
- What metaphors or analogies do narrators or interviewees use to explain Jobs and his impact?

Key Points and Storytelling Critique of Steve Jobs's Speech

The key points found in each story are as follows:

- ◎ *Story 1*: Trust in something, follow where it leads you, and you will be able to connect the dots in your life as you look back.

- ◎ *Story 2*: Love what you do, as it will enable you to do great work. Great work leads to satisfaction in life as well as in all other matters of the heart.

- ◎ *Story 3*: Life is brief; don't waste the time you are given by following someone else's expectations for you.

Handout 3.1

Biographical Chart: Steve Jobs

Full Name: _____

Lifespan: _____

Early Family Background and Created Family Structure

_____

_____

_____

Personality Characteristics and Areas of Aptitude, Talent, and Interest

_____

_____

_____

Major Career/Professional Events and Accomplishments

_____

_____

_____

Personal Life Themes/Beliefs

_____

_____

_____

Selected Quotations

_____

_____

_____

Awards and Recognition

_____

_____

_____

_____

Name: _____ Date: _____

Leadership Storytelling Checklist

Story Elements

◎ A story has a beginning, middle, and end.

◎ A scene or setting for the story (where and when) is described.

◎ A story has a main character or protagonist.

◎ A story has an arc, such as a predicament or problem faced or a change undertaken.

◎ The intentions or motivations are made clear or tacitly understood by the listener.

◎ The story has relevance to the larger point being made.

Criteria for an Effective Story

◎ The story has all or most of the elements needed to make a story.

◎ The story is clear.

◎ The story is comprehensive.

◎ The story is compelling.

Handout 3.3

Key Points and Storytelling Critique of Steve Jobs's Speech

Story 1's Key Point:	
❑ Has all or most of the elements ❑ Is clear ❑ Is comprehensive ❑ Is compelling	Explain any boxes that were unchecked:
Story 2's Key Point:	
❑ Has all or most of the elements ❑ Is clear ❑ Is comprehensive ❑ Is compelling	Explain any boxes that were unchecked:
Story 3's Key Point:	
❑ Has all or most of the elements ❑ Is clear ❑ Is comprehensive ❑ Is compelling	Explain any boxes that were unchecked:

Handout 3.4
Journal Entry Questions

1. What did you learn from the biographical study of Steve Jobs that is particularly illuminating in your understanding of leadership? In what ways is Steve Jobs a role model for you and other emerging leaders?

2. In his Stanford speech, Jobs talks about the intersection of art and science in the design of the Macintosh computer. In what other areas of his work or in what other gadgets that he pioneered do you see evidence of the interdependence of these two domains? Cite two or three examples and explain the points of integration.

3. (Only answer this question if you uncovered an error on a site.) What mistakes or misinformation did you uncover in any of the Internet sites that you investigated on Steve Jobs's biography? How do you know if the information you have examined is consistently accurate? Where would you go next if you wanted to learn about Mr. Jobs's life in more depth?

4. The effective use of storytelling as a motivational strategy pervades much of recent literature dealing with the topic of leadership. What did you learn about the use of storytelling for this end that you may not have understood or considered before? How do you think one develops the capacity for effective storytelling? Who do you know who is a good storyteller and why?

Lesson 4
Dwight D. Eisenhower and Team Building

Leadership is the art of getting someone else to do something you want done because he wants to do it.

—Dwight D. Eisenhower

Instructional Purpose

- ◎ To practice using the Internet to do biographical research
- ◎ To map biographical data against key leadership factors
- ◎ To experience and analyze how group dynamics affect team building in leadership

Materials Needed

- ◎ Handout 4.1: Biographical Chart: Dwight D. Eisenhower
- ◎ Sufficient numbers of the following materials to give each small group in the class its own set:
  - o two sheets of typing paper
  - o one role of tape
  - o two felt-tip markers
  - o one pair of scissors
  - o five large Styrofoam cups
  - o two paper plates (not Styrofoam)
  - o four sheets of construction paper
  - o two pipe cleaners

- ◎ Handout 4.2: Definition and Characteristics of Effective Teams
- ◎ Handout 4.3: Journal Entry Questions
- ◎ Teachers' Rap Sheet on Dwight D. Eisenhower (see Appendix A)

Activities and Instructional Strategies

Part I (1 period)

1. In the homework assignment for the previous lesson, students were directed to the Internet to collect biographical data on Dwight D. Eisenhower, President of the United States from 1953–1961 and five-star general in the United States Armed Forces. Ask students who in their fam-

ily was alive during the Eisenhower administration. Ask: Approximately how old was that person at that time?

2. For an alternative to doing this as homework, see Part I of Lesson 2. If this research is done at the beginning of class, be sure to set the context for the study of President Eisenhower, as he is the first biographical figure who is not a contemporary of the students. (See the Homework section in Lesson 3 for information.)

3. The teacher will have the whole class complete a master Biographical Chart on Dwight D. Eisenhower, based on the information students found from completing their research. This should be done using a white board or overhead projector. The teacher will start by asking: What did you discover about our former President's early family background and created family structure? What did you discover about his education? Follow this format until the chart has been completed. The teacher may choose to annotate the information collected by drawing on the Teachers' Rap Sheet for President Eisenhower if students have failed to grasp and/ or record important pieces of biographical information.

4. An option for the completion of the master chart is to again use small groups to aggregate the information as was done in Lesson 3. If this approach is used, the teacher might ask questions to ensure that salient information was found, such as: What in Dwight Eisenhower's early background stands out? Describe his succession of promotions in the military and explain what accounted for the speed at which he attained the highest rank. What do you think was the most important honor he received in his lifetime?

Part II (1 period)

1. The teacher will engage students in a large-group discussion using the following questions:
   o In what ways was Dwight D. Eisenhower a leader? (Probe for justification as needed.) How is leadership in the military the same as or different from leadership in business? How is leadership in politics the same as or different from leadership in business? How is leadership in the military the same as or different from leadership in politics?
   o To what extent did time, place, and circumstances impact his ability to become a leader?
   o How would you describe the vision that General Eisenhower brought to his military career? How would you describe his vision for his tenure as President of the United States following the aftermath of World War II?

- What evidence is there of initiative, perseverance, and risk taking in Dwight D. Eisenhower's profile? Did you find any evidence that he had a sense of humor?
- What other personal characteristics contributed to President Eisenhower's notable success in both the military and in politics? What common and what different skill sets did he need to succeed in both of these fields? In what ways did he evidence personal growth over the span of his life?
- What do you see as President Eisenhower's lasting impact and contributions during his career in the military, his roles following his discharge from the military, and his tenure as President? What innovations and/or improvements can you credit him with championing? How has the passage of time impacted President's Eisenhower's legacy?
- President Eisenhower said: "If a problem cannot be solved, enlarge it." What do you think he meant by this? Can you give an example of a problem that must be given a broader scope in order to find a solution that will address it? Do you think the converse is true (i.e., if a problem cannot be solved, reduce it to smaller pieces)?

2. If you were President Eisenhower's (Ike) campaign manager in 1956 when he ran for reelection, what would you suggest for his campaign slogan? ("I like Ike" has already been taken.) (Allow students a few minutes to think about their answers to this question.)

Part III (1+ period).

The following exercise was adapted from *The Team-Building Workshop* by Vivette Payne (2001).

1. Divide the class into groups of 4–5 students. Do not use the word *team* as you are doing Steps 1–5. You may need to move desks around to give groups space to perform the task. Give the groups the following oral instructions: You are going to do a project together. I am going to distribute the following materials to each of your groups:
   - two sheets of typing paper,
   - one role of tape,
   - two felt-tip markers,
   - one pair of scissors,
   - five large Styrofoam cups,
   - two paper plates (not Styrofoam),
   - four sheets of construction paper, and
   - two pipe cleaners.

Each group is going to use these materials to construct an art object. You need to create a sculpture or statue that is at least 5 feet high and freestanding (it cannot be taped to the floor). It will be evaluated on two criteria: (a) Does it meet the height requirement? and (b) Is the design creative? You will have 10 minutes to plan your object and 20 minutes to build it. I will start timing once all of the materials are distributed. Are there any questions?

2. Distribute the materials and instruct the groups to begin planning their artwork. After 10 minutes, let them know the planning period is over and they should begin building.
3. Give the group a time warning after 15 minutes. After 20 minutes, instruct them to stop.
4. Ask each group to describe its art object. Measure to determine if it meets the 5-foot requirement using a student around that height. Verify that each sculpture is freestanding.
5. Congratulate the groups on their creativity and ingenuity in responding to the criteria.
6. Reseat students and ask the class for a definition of the word *team*. After exploring several responses, distribute Handout 4.2: Characteristics of Effective Teams and give them a minute to digest its contents. Ask students to think about whether they operated as a team in performing the task assigned.
7. Use the following prompts to help students reflect on their participation in the group work and allow one or two students to comment as appropriate:
   o Was everyone on your team actively involved in both the planning process and the building process, or did you stratify roles?
   o Who worked to see that everyone was included in some part of the task?
   o Did someone emerge as a group leader? Did leadership rotate as the phases changed or was it a shared process with equal levels of participation?
   o Who influenced the discussion most? Who influenced the physical construction most?
   o Who was most motivated to carry the task through to the end?
   o How well did team members cooperate with one another? Was there competition within the team?
   o What process was used to agree on a design for the art object?

   o Did the artwork gradually evolve or did it change radically during the construction phase? Who championed the changes? Who resisted them?

   o Eisenhower said: "In preparing for battle I have always found that plans are useless, but planning is indispensable." What did he mean by this? How does his axiom apply here?

   o What did you learn about your own behavior in doing this exercise? Would you have done anything differently if I had told you the purpose was to see how well you work in a team with an open-ended project?

Part IV (1 period or less)

1. Distribute Handout 4.3: Journal Entry Questions to students and allow them 15–20 minutes to select at least two and complete their journal entries. As an option, you may assign specific questions to individuals or to the whole class.
2. After the time has elapsed, ask for some volunteers to share their responses and discuss the questions as a whole class.
3. This part may also be done as homework as long as there is sufficient time between this class and the next one for the biographical research on the next leader to be completed.

Assessment

The teacher should check to see that each student has completed two written pieces for the implementation of the lesson: Handout 4.1 (unless assigned as a group project) and the journal entry.

Homework

Students are assigned responsibility for completing Handout 5.1: Biographical Chart: Thurgood Marshall in preparation for the next class period. The three sites that students should be directed to for conducting this research are as follows:

   ◎ Biography.com (http://www.biography.com/people/thurgood-marshall-9400241; the website includes a 47-minute video for students to view along with reading the biography)

   ◎ Wikipedia (http://en.wikipedia.org/wiki/Thurgood_Marshall)

   ◎ *Justice for All: The Legacy of Thurgood Marshall* (http://America.gov/media/pdf/books/marshall.pdf)

The third site, which directs students to a PDF on Marshall, offers a number of articles on Thurgood Marshall and gives interesting details about his role in setting up the first legal framework for Kenya after it achieved its independence. This site may be omitted if there is a concern about time.

In addition, the teacher should set the stage by pointing out that Thurgood Marshall was only one generation younger than Dwight D. Eisenhower but that they were contemporaries during much of the early and middle 20th century.

Extensions

The following ideas are offered as substitutions for parts of the above lesson or as extensions for this lesson focusing on Dwight D. Eisenhower and the practice of team building in leadership.

◎ Present the following as a mini-lecture. Dwight D. Eisenhower received his leadership training in the United States military. In a book by William A. Cohen (2008), the author discussed the two basic assumptions on which training in the armed services rests. He noted that these two assumptions date back to the much-admired Spartans who began training warriors at age 7 and continued for 12 years. The Spartans required everyone to serve in the military, and they trained year round. According to Cohen,

> The first assumption is that the harder you train, the easier the actual military actions would be and the better your performance. George Patton, WWII General, put it this way: *A pint of sweat in training is worth a gallon of blood in combat.*
>
> The second assumption is that even the lowest ranking private has the capability of reaching the highest levels of responsibility and command. The old saying is that "in every private's knapsack, there is a marshal's baton." This practice is an absolute necessity because on the battlefield, officers and non-commissioned officers must sometimes be replaced immediately, without warning or additional training. This means that everyone has to be prepared at all times to assume higher responsibilities. (pp. 177–178)

Share this information with students and then break them into small groups to discuss the following questions:

○ How do these assumptions about how to train people relate to the concept of leadership? In other words, what ideas or behaviors of military leaders might evolve or flow from these assumptions?

- o Do these assumptions for military training have relevance beyond the military? Explain why or why not and give some applications if you think so.
- o What implications do these assumptions have for the practice of team building?
- o Would K–12 education look different if these assumptions were the basis for its design? How so?
- o What assumptions can you state that underlie your educational program at this school? What relationship do these assumptions have to the development of leadership abilities in students?

Reconvene the whole class and debrief as a large group.

◎ Direct students to the website for the Kansas Heritage Group (http://www.kansasheritage.org) and have them read two documents: The D-Day Fact Sheet for June 6, 1944 Normandy, France (http://www.kansasheritage.org/abilene/ikedday.html) and General Dwight D. Eisenhower (Ike) D-Day Message Order of the Day: 6 June 1944 (http://www.kansasheritage.org/abilene/ikespeech.html). These are both very brief but historically powerful. Ask them to draft responses to the following three probes:
- o What is the vision that Eisenhower creates for his troops in this brief statement?
- o What values does he remind them they possess to see the task through?
- o What lessons can one derive about team building from examining the speech and the context and aftermath of its delivery?

   Reconvene the whole class to debrief responses. The first two questions require little time, but the third question opens up more opportunity for discussion and extrapolation.

◎ Of the speeches he gave as President, Eisenhower is most remembered for his warning about the proliferation of the military-industrial complex that he foreshadowed in his farewell address to the American people (January 17, 1961) as he exited office. The full text of this speech can be found online (http://www.informationclearinghouse.info/article5407.htm) and the video can be viewed on YouTube. Have students examine this material, orally summarize the main points he makes in the speech as a whole group, and then respond individually to the following three questions in writing:
- o How effective is this speech as a farewell address from the President to the people of his country? Explain or justify your assessment.

o Can the people of a country ever be considered as a team? If yes, under what circumstances is this most likely to occur? If no, why not?

o What relevance does an understanding of team building have to the office of the President of the United States?

Name: _____ Date: _____

Biographical Chart: Dwight D. Eisenhower

Full Name: _____

Lifespan: _____

Early Family Background and Created Family Structure

_____

_____

_____

Personality Characteristics and Areas of Aptitude, Talent, and Interest

_____

_____

_____

Major Career/Professional Events and Accomplishments

_____

_____

_____

Personal Life Themes/Beliefs

_____

_____

_____

Selected Quotations

_____

_____

_____

Awards and Recognition

_____

_____

_____

_____

Handout 4.2

Definition and Characteristics of Effective Teams

(Adapted from *Successful Team Building* by Thomas L. Quick)

Team: A group of interdependent individuals who have complementary skills and are committed to a shared, meaningful vision and specific goals.

Indicators of Effective Teams

◎ Approach to work is collaborative with free flow and sharing of information.

◎ Interpersonal relationships are characterized by trust, respect, and mutual support.

◎ Conflict is understood as helpful and evolves from issues, not personalities.

◎ Atmosphere created is nonthreatening and encourages participation.

◎ The decision process is open and promotes consensus.

◎ Power derives from competence and contributions made.

◎ Members are internally motivated.

◎ Rewards are based on performance of the team rather than the individual.

Handout 4.3
Journal Entry Questions

1. What did you learn from the biographical study of President Eisenhower that is particularly illuminating in your understanding of leadership? In what ways is President Eisenhower a role model for you and other emerging leaders? Which other Presidents in the last 60 years do you think have influenced your generation of young leaders and in what ways?

2. President Eisenhower got his formal training and much of his experience in leadership in the U.S. Armed Forces. Do you think the military has an effective system for developing leadership skills in general (no pun intended)? What specific leadership skill set is the military well suited to develop? Do you think military training crosses over into other walks of life, such as education, politics, and technology? Why or why not?

3. We have repeated a pattern in this class in our approach to studying leadership. First, we read the biographical information about a specific leader, then we process it as a large or small group to see that everyone understands the important elements in that leader's life. Then we have a large-group discussion relating to the linkages between that person's life and what we know about the topic of leadership. Next, we have an application exercise related to one or more of the generalizations we are studying. We have now studied three leaders using this format and have three to go. How effective is this format and what changes would you recommend? Do you have suggestions for other questions that we should be including in the large-group discussion about the linkages between the person (representative) and the topic (leadership)?

4. Every important contribution relies on the talents of multiple players. Even great works that are created individually (e.g., novels, paintings, inventions, equations) must rely on the involvement of other people to get that product to a market or audience. What have you learned about teamwork so far that relates to leadership? How do you think one develops a capacity for both working on a team and for managing a team?

Lesson 5
Thurgood Marshall and Conflict Resolution

....

Our whole constitutional heritage rebels at the thought of giving government the power to control men's minds.

—Thurgood Marshall

Instructional Purpose

- ◎ To practice using the Internet to do biographical research
- ◎ To map biographical data against key leadership factors
- ◎ To evaluate how one deals with conflict and to understand different approaches to conflict resolution

Materials Needed

- ◎ Handout 5.1: Biographical Chart: Thurgood Marshall
- ◎ Handout 5.2: Swing Vote Decisions
- ◎ Handout 5.3: Understanding Conflict
- ◎ Handout 5.4: Conflict Management Styles
- ◎ Handout 5.5: Journal Entry Questions
- ◎ Teachers' Rap Sheet on Thurgood Marshall (see Appendix A)

Activities and Instructional Strategies

Part I (1 period if homework has been completed)

1. In the homework assignment for the previous lesson, students were directed to the Internet to collect biographical data on Thurgood Marshall, Supreme Court Justice and titan of the American Civil Rights Movement. (This is the first biography for which students are expected to glean much of the information from viewing a video.) Ask students if they remember when the case of *Brown v. Board of Education* was decided by the Supreme Court (1954). Ask them to calculate how old Marshall was at that time and how old Eisenhower was then. For alternatives to doing the research as homework or for doing only portions of the Biographical Chart, see Part I of Lesson 2. If this is done at the beginning of class, the teacher may choose to omit the second and/or third websites, as there will not be sufficient time to have students watch the video and visit the text-based sites as well.

2. Group students into groups of 4–5 and have them create master charts on Thurgood Marshall using the information collected by each student. As they review their charts, advise them to add any important points that have not been recorded but that they remember from reading the material. After allowing 30–35 minutes for this, ask the groups some questions that will ensure that they have retrieved some of the most salient information about Mr. Marshall. Sample questions are as follows:

   o What kind of a childhood did Thurgood Marshall have? How would you describe his educational experiences? In what areas did he excel during high school?

   o What precipitated his interest in the field of law?

   o What were some of the jobs he held before his appointment to the Supreme Court of the United States?

   o What was the case of *Brown v. Board of Education* about? What was Marshall's role in this case? Why is it considered a landmark case?

   o What do you think was the most important award given to Justice Marshall?

3. The teacher may choose to annotate the information collected by drawing on the Teachers' Rap Sheet for Mr. Marshall if students have failed to grasp and/or record important pieces of biographical information.

4. Conclude this part of the lesson by pointing out that both Eisenhower and Marshall were intelligent, articulate, and well-educated men, but their respective races impacted their experiences of American culture. Ask students who they think was more race-conscious during the post-World War II era and why.

Part II (1 period)

1. The teacher will engage students in a large-group discussion using the following questions:

   o In what ways was Thurgood Marshall a leader? (Probe for justification if needed.) Can you compare and contrast leadership in legal and judicial fields with other areas we have studied? How so?

   o To what extent did time, place, and circumstances impact his ability to become a leader?

   o How would you describe the perspective that Justice Marshall brought to his tenure on the Supreme Court (i.e., was he a strict Constitutionalist or did he see the court as an architect of social change)? Justify or explain your answer. In what ways is judicial perspective similar to or different from the concept of vision? How would you describe

Marshall's vision for the Civil Rights Movement in the United States? Did he live to see his vision realized?

o What evidence is there of initiative, perseverance, and risk taking in Justice Marshall's profile?

o What other personal characteristics contributed to Thurgood Marshall's record-breaking success as a lawyer and in his role on the Supreme Court? In what ways, if any, did Justice Marshall evidence personal growth or change over the course of his life?

o What do you see as Justice Marshall's lasting impact and contributions in the arena of jurisprudence? What government policies and/or legal decisions did he contribute to that shaped or changed our society for the better? Were his contributions as seminal as those of Martin Luther King, Jr.'s? Why or why not?

o Justice Marshall said: "History teaches that grave threats to liberty often come in times of urgency, when constitutional rights seem too extravagant to endure." What did he mean by this? This statement was often quoted after 9/11 when federal laws were being changed to reduce the degree of privacy that American citizens had experienced until the terrorist attack on American soil. How would Marshall have advised the President and Congress in regards to protecting citizen rights versus ensuring citizen safety? What are the consequences of going too far in one direction or the other?

o Ask: If you had to design a logo or graphic to symbolize the ideas of justice and equality, what would you create? Explain why you chose that image or symbol. (Give students a few minutes to think about their answers to this question.)

Part III (1 period)

1. The initial part of Part III of this lesson is designed to fool students into thinking the lesson is about one topic when in fact it is about another. The teacher will need an accomplice to carry out the ruse. The teacher may enlist the help of one or two students prior to the onset of class and explain their roles to them. Or, the teacher might have an adult, such as the principal, assist in creating a staged conflict. If the teacher uses students to assist in the lesson, the teacher will need to tell them the following:

> I need your help in implementing the next part of our study of Thurgood Marshall. In order to help me, you must agree not to tell your classmates what is going on. I am going to give the class a set of instructions for a task to carry out while I

step out of the room. I will ask for a volunteer to facilitate the class discussion while I am gone in order to get the assignment done quickly. I want you to raise questions or hinder the attempts of the class to reach consensus in order to delay and prevent the assignment from getting done while I am gone. Challenge the person in charge regarding his or her role in leading the class. Disagree with ideas that are being put forth. If the class votes to do one thing, say there should be a minority group effort to do another thing. Don't be so obvious that the other students will know what you are up to but try to get people anxious about getting the assignment done before I return. The real purpose of the lesson is for students to see for themselves how they react to a conflictive situation without knowing they are being set up for one.

2. To start the lesson, the teacher should distribute Handout 5.2: Swing Vote Decisions and go over the background information on the handout with students. Point out the categories that the five swing vote examples cover. Tell the class that the assignment is to select one of the decisions that was decided by a 5-4 vote on the Supreme Court and to think of arguments that would support the opposite outcome. Tell them that you have to step out of the room to handle some problem in the office or to make an emergency phone call and you need a student to facilitate the discussion. You will be back in 15 minutes and in that time they need to have picked one case by getting a consensus decision and identified at least three potential arguments/reasons that could be researched to support a reverse decision. Tell them that this part of the lesson must be done quickly in order to get to the next part. Apologize for having to leave the class but assure the students you have confidence in their ability to cooperate to get the task done speedily.

3. Stay within earshot of the door to the class and reenter when it is clear that students are frustrated that some of their classmates are sabotaging the assignment (stay outside no longer than 8 minutes). Act surprised that they are not further along in getting the task done and ask for an explanation of why. As the perceptions about the sequence of events unfold, ask students for a definition of the word *conflict*. After some suggestions are put forth, ask them if they had any emotional reactions to the situation that transpired. Were they nervous, surprised, agitated, or detached?

4. If the above scenario will not work in your situation, you can create an alternative situation using another staff member who interrupts the assignment with some bogus issue and challenges your authority in the

classroom. Or, you can skip this manufactured experience and go directly to the next component of the lesson, omitting the use of Handout 5.2 altogether.

5. Tell the class that this part of the lesson deals with the issue of conflict and with approaches to conflict management. Point out that the third generalization posits that leadership recognizes the inevitability of conflict but uses conflict to sharpen ideas and transform resistance. Ask students why it is important that leaders understand conflict and know how to use it or diffuse it. Distribute Handout 5.3: Understanding Conflict and Handout 5.4: Conflict Management Styles. Review Handout 5.3 with the large group.

6. Break the class into small groups to discuss Handout 5.4. Tell them their first task is to identify situations in which the use of each of these styles may be called for, one example for each style. Their second task is to examine more closely the use of the collaborative style in order to create win-win situations. Clarify that they understand the term *win-win*. Their second task is to identify three things that people can do to approach conflict resolution from a win-win vantage point. Tell students that one of Stephen Covey's (2004) seven habits of highly effective people is to "Seek first to understand, then to be understood."

7. Reconvene the whole class and debrief some of the ideas that students proposed in their small-group discussions.

Part IV (1 period or less)

1. Distribute Handout 5.5: Journal Entry Questions to students and allow them 15–20 minutes to select at least two and complete their journal entries. As an option, you may assign specific questions to individuals or to the whole class.

2. After the time has elapsed, ask for some volunteers to share their responses and discuss the questions as a whole class.

3. This part may also be done as homework as long as there is sufficient time between this class and the next one for the biographical research on the next leader to be completed. Another option is to create small groups and assign each group two of the four questions, ensuring there is enough overlap so that all questions are covered but each group has a different combination.

Assessment

The teacher should check to see that each student has completed the Biographical Chart on Thurgood Marshall and prepared written responses for the journal entry (if journal questions are done in a small group, make copies of each group's work for inclusion in student portfolios but label it as "group work").

Homework

Students are assigned responsibility for completing Handout 7.1: Biographical Chart: Maya Lin in preparation for Lesson 7. The five sites that students should be directed to for conducting this research are as follows (note that two of the sites require them to view short videos):
- Wikipedia (http://en.wikipedia.org/wiki/Maya_Lin)
- Stanford Presidential Lectures and Symposia in the Humanities and Arts (http://prelectur.stanford.edu/lecturers/lin/)
- Academy of Achievement (http://www.achievement.org/autodoc/page/lin0pro-1 and http://www.achievement.org/autodoc/page/lin0int-1; read the profile and the transcript of the interview with Lin)
- Art21 (http://www.pbs.org/art21/artists/maya-lin; watch the 11-minute video interview)
- YouTube.com (http://www.youtube.com/watch?v=l38Ea10sNBI; a 4-minute video of an interview with Maya Lin)

Extensions

The following ideas are offered as substitutions for parts of the above lesson or as extensions for this lesson focusing on Thurgood Marshall and the art of conflict management in leadership.
- Thurgood Marshall gave a commencement address to the students of the University of Virginia on May 21, 1978. The full text of this is not available online, and the abbreviated version on the University of Virginia's website does not do the speech justice. The text of the speech is available in *Thurgood Marshall: His Speeches, Writings, Arguments, Opinions, and Reminiscences* (Tushnet, 2001). Obtain a copy of the speech and have students read it and then write a paper addressing the following four prompts:
  - Summarize the elements of the vision for higher education that Marshall ascribes to Thomas Jefferson.
  - Describe the core values that Marshall cites in the body of his speech and his take-away advice to the student assemblage.
  - Describe the point made in the Jobs's commencement address that has echoes of the point made in Marshall's address. (Hint: It is near the end of both speeches.)

- Critique the effectiveness of Marshall's speech from your point of view regarding leadership.

- Juan Williams is the author of an excellent biography of Marshall entitled *Thurgood Marshall: American Revolutionary* (2000). There is a one-hour video interview with Williams conducted by Brian Lamb (http://booknotes.org/Watch/111331-1/Juan+Williams.aspx) that contains interesting anecdotes and commentary about Marshall's life and the judicial and political personalities that surrounded him. Have students listen to the interview (a transcript is also provided) and answer the following questions either in writing or orally:
  - How has your understanding of Thurgood Marshall changed as a result of listening to this interview?
  - Who were and what was Marshall's connection to or interaction with the following individuals: Charlie Houston, Langston Hughes, Robert Kennedy, William O. Douglas, and Malcolm X?
  - What example can you cite in which Marshall had to take a position as a legal advocate that differed from his personal perspective on an issue?
  - Williams says in the interview that Marshall "restructured the terms on which we consider and argue and think about race in America." What does he mean by this assertion? Do you agree or disagree and why?

- Have students read the three speeches of Marshall's that are posted on the website for Juan William's (2000) book, *Thurgood Marshall: American Revolutionary* (http://thurgoodmarshall.com). These speeches are entitled The Equality Speech, The Bicentennial Speech, and The Sword and Robe. Have them write a paper first describing what they learned about Marshall's perceptions in two areas: judicial perspective and racial issues in America. Next, have them comment on the impact of these speeches on their understanding and/or appreciation of Marshall's leadership abilities and legacy.

Handout 5.1

Biographical Chart: Thurgood Marshall

Full Name: _____

Lifespan: _____

Early Family Background and Created Family Structure

_____

_____

_____

Personality Characteristics and Areas of Aptitude, Talent, and Interest

_____

_____

_____

Major Career/Professional Events and Accomplishments

_____

_____

_____

Personal Life Themes/Beliefs

_____

_____

_____

Selected Quotations

_____

_____

_____

Awards and Recognition

_____

_____

_____

_____

Swing Vote Decisions

Background

Between 1900 and 1950, a one-vote majority decided only 4% of Supreme Court decisions. By 1969, the average had climbed to 18%. In the 2006 and 2008 terms, the Roberts court set a new record with about one in three cases being decided by a single swing vote. More recently, this has dropped to 18% or less (Kuhn, 2010).

Five Recent Examples of Cases Decided by a Swing Vote

- **Private School Vouchers** (*Zelman v. Simmons-Harris* in 2002): The Court affirmed the school voucher program in Ohio for low-income parents that allowed these parents to send their children to religiously affiliated schools, saying it was not a violation of the First Amendment (separation of church and state).
- **Racial Preferences in College Admissions** (*Grutter v. Bollinger* in 2003): The Court affirmed that the University of Michigan Law School could use racial preference to include Blacks, Latinos, and Indians in its incoming class because of the educational benefits associated with having a "critical mass" of minorities in the student body.
- **Religious Displays** (*McCreary County v. ACLU of Kentucky* in 2005): The Court disallowed the display of copies of the Ten Commandments in the courtrooms of two Kentucky counties because the displays had an overt religious purpose and the First Amendment requires government to be neutral.
- **Gun Ownership** (*McDonald et al. v. City of Chicago, IL* in 2010): The Court struck down a local ordinance restricting gun ownership, indicating that state and local governments cannot violate a citizen's Second Amendment rights (right to bear arms), but it does not extend to all potential gun control laws.
- **Patient Protection and Affordable Care Act** (*National Federation of Independent Business, et al. v. Sebelius, Secretary of Health and Human Services, et al.* in 2012): The Court affirmed that the health care overhaul signed into law under President Obama was constitutional in requiring that most Americans obtain health insurance or pay a penalty based on the authority of Congress to levy taxes. Chief Justice John Roberts sided with the four liberal members of the Court in a ruling that was described by the *New York Times* as the most significant federalism decision since the New Deal. Opponents of the legislation had argued that federal government does not have the authority to require people to purchase commodities that they do not want to buy even though the government under the Interstate Commerce Act can regulate economic activity across state lines.

Reference

Kuhn, D. P. (2010). *The polarization of the Supreme Court.* Retrieved from http://www. realclearpolitics.com/articles/2010/07/02/the_polarization_of_the_supreme_court_ john_roberts_elana_kagan_106176.html

Name: _____ Date: _____

Understanding Conflict
(Adapted from *The Team-Building Workshop* by Vivette Payne)

Potential Outcomes of Constructive Conflict

◎ Opens up and clarifies issues

◎ Helps to resolve problems and move parties forward

◎ Discloses new information and perspectives

◎ Promotes authentic and empathic communication

◎ Facilitates team learning and individual participant growth

◎ Assists in generating breakthroughs, creativity, and innovative thinking

Potential Outcomes of Destructive Conflict

◎ Saps energy and diminishes morale

◎ Polarizes participants and deepens differences

◎ Delays team problem solving and hampers individual growth

Name: _____ Date: _____

Conflict Management Styles
(Adapted from *The Team-Building Workshop* by Vivette Payne)

Direct Style: You seek to control people or situations. You want to overcome opposition and pursue your own interests and needs. You approach conflictive situations by:
- defending your position,
- trying to win,
- seeking an immediate solution or resolution,
- taking charge,
- using authority of position or role to eliminate differences, and
- arguing your position forcefully.

Avoidance Style: You tend to be passive and withdraw in conflictive situations. You prefer to sidestep issues or postpone confronting them, hoping they'll work themselves out. You approach conflictive situations by:
- not showing up for events in which you expect conflict to develop or by tuning out as it unfolds;
- letting others take responsibility for dealing with the conflict;
- denying, ignoring, or accepting the situation; and
- suppressing your own needs and feelings.

Collaborative Style: You desire to stand up for your own needs but use a proactive approach to engaging others in collaboration to find a solution that everyone can live with and support. You approach conflictive situations by:
- seeking to identify underlying issues and concerns,
- offering creative and innovative alternatives,
- working toward win-win solutions,
- viewing conflict as an opportunity for growth rather than as a problem,
- encouraging others to work together, and
- helping others to verbalize their concerns.

Accommodation Style: You desire to maintain harmonious relationships even if it means sacrificing what you really want for the good of the group. You tend to cooperate readily, are often selfless, and yield to others' points of view. You approach conflictive situations by:
- acting conciliatory,
- using empathic listening skills,
- assisting others in getting what they want,
- trying to maintain a harmonious environment,
- respecting or deferring to all points of view, and
- minimizing your ability to influence the outcome.

Handout 5.5
Journal Entry Questions

1. What did you learn from the biographical study of Thurgood Marshall that is particularly illuminating in your understanding of leadership? In what ways is Thurgood Marshall a role model for you and other emerging leaders?

2. Many social scientists would suggest that racial relations have represented the most prevalent endemic conflict in the history of the United States including the last half century. Do you think this continues to be true or not since the election of the first African American president? Justify or explain the position you are taking in regards to this query.

3. Our seventh generalization states that "Leadership requires strong beliefs and clearly defined values and the passion and tenacity to act in accordance with them." Describe how this generalization applies to Thurgood Marshall. How does his life story illustrate his beliefs and values, how did he embody them in his choices and actions, and how did he impact the beliefs and values of others?

4. How do you handle conflict? What kinds of visceral reactions do you experience when you are in a conflictive situation? What did you learn about constructive or healthy conflict and about conflict management from this lesson that you did not know before? How do you think one develops or hones conflict resolution and conflict management skills?

Lesson 6
Distinctions in Roles and Leadership Generalizations Revisited

Instructional Purpose

- ◎ To examine conceptual distinctions between managers and leaders
- ◎ To apply unit generalizations to the leaders studied to date
- ◎ To prepare questions for use with the panel of leaders in Lesson 9
- ◎ To complete the Leadership Self-Assessment Inventory

Materials Needed

- ◎ Handout 6.1: List of Suggested Differences Between Managers and Leaders
- ◎ Handout 6.2: Leadership Generalizations Matrix
- ◎ Handout 6.3: Master Roster of Panel Questions
- ◎ Handout 6.4: Leadership Self-Assessment Inventory

Activities and Instructional Strategies

Part I (20–30 minutes)

1. Ask students what they think the role of a manager in an organization is and get them to list some responsibilities of a manager. If they need some prompting, get them to give examples of a manager (e.g., a person who oversees a large store, a person in charge of a large project, a principal of a school building, a supervisor for a shift of workers at a manufacturing plant). Prompt them to see that managers have responsibility for two interdependent elements: people and tasks (basic management theory).

2. Ask students to think like a manager for a few minutes. What are some different ways that a manager might think about classifying the people under his or her purview (e.g., trained, untrained; highly motivated, unmotivated; cooperative, challenging)? Then ask students to suggest some ways for classifying tasks in an organization (e.g., individual, group; skilled, unskilled; simple, complex; short term, long term). Ask students to describe a successful manager in light of this understanding of the manager's role.

3. Ask students if managers are leaders. After several ideas have been proposed, tell them that leaders often have management skills and that managers often have leadership skills, but current leadership theory makes distinctions between these two roles. Distribute Handout 6.1: List of Suggested Differences Between Managers and Leaders and review some of the distinctions presented.

4. Ask students if they find these ideas useful in understanding the concept of leadership. Then ask if these ideas have more relevance for some domains and fields than others (i.e., where do these distinctions seem most appropriate?). Wrap up this part of the lesson by asking which, if any, of the four leaders studied so far has demonstrated the differences in these two roles and in what way? Where can they illustrate overlap in roles?

5. Tell students that the next part of this lesson will revisit the generalizations that were proposed in Lesson 1 to see how they hold up when mapped against the leaders studied to date.

Part II (35–40 minutes)

1. Tell students that they have examined and discussed the life stories of four leaders so far in this unit: two in the business sector (one of them in technology; the other in entertainment), one who represented both the military and politics, and one from the legal/judiciary field. They have studied three men and one woman: two Whites and two African Americans. The assignment for this part of the lesson is to analyze how a subset of these four leaders illustrates three of the generalizations that were proposed at the beginning of the unit. Distribute Handout 6.2: Leadership Generalizations Matrix and go over the instructions. Tell students they will have 20 minutes to complete the assignment and ask if there are any questions. After 18 minutes, give a 2-minute warning.

2. Go over each generalization and ask for students to share their responses. Allow for questions, observations, and disagreements by other students. Play devil's advocate to ensure that students can justify their answers. If the thinking shown by students has been shallow, get them to make more sophisticated connections. If a particular leader has been overlooked by a group of students, ask them to make oral responses on that leader's application to the generalizations.

3. Collect their individual work and review it after class for a sense of their level of analysis of the ideas. Give them a check mark if the work is satisfactory, a check plus if it is exemplary, and a check minus if it is incomplete. Return it within the next two class periods.

4. Wrap up this part of the lesson by asking if any other generalizations about leadership have evolved from their study and analysis to date. Put their ideas on the board. Explore and process these ideas as appropriate. Ask if any assumptions or preconceptions they held about leadership before they started the unit have been changed or modified. These questions should help stimulate their thinking for the next part of the lesson.

Part III (40 minutes)

1. At this point in the unit, the arrangements for the composition of the panel in Lesson 9 should be completed. Confirm with students who is coming or announce to them the panel makeup. Tell them that each panel participant will be given 3–5 minutes to describe his or her job and where it fits into the organizational structure in which the panelist operates. (Allow more time if there are fewer than four people on the panel). The rest of the panel's time will be devoted to the class's questions to the panel. Most of the questions will be tightly structured, but there will also be some time for spontaneous questions that arise from the information that is shared by panel participants. The goal in this part of the lesson is to create an agreed-upon set of questions based on the students' interest in and understanding of leadership to date.

2. Break the class into small groups (no more than five groups) to develop questions for the panel members. Have them record and edit their questions and be ready to share them with the whole class. After 20 minutes, reconvene the class.

3. Distribute Handout 6.3: Master Roster of Panel Questions to all students to use for note taking once the whole class has been reconvened. Have the first group share the questions it developed. Have the whole class vote on which of these questions should be put on the roster for the panel discussion. Ask if there are any suggested edits to the questions that are voted onto the roster. Have a student volunteer create an official, legible copy of Handout 6.3 as decisions are made regarding questions so that you will have a copy. Repeat the process with subsequent groups, but caution them to avoid duplication by omitting questions from their oral reports that have already been put on the master roster. If a student reporter fails to follow this instruction, remind the class of the importance of listening skills.

4. Ask for volunteers to raise each question on the day of the panel presentation. Make assignments accordingly. Add the questioner's name to the roster. After class, make copies of the master roster for each student. Distribute the copies of the master roster on the day of the panel.

5. Before concluding this component of the lesson, remind students that they can also ask spontaneous questions and to be thinking about other important issues that come to mind as they continue to study the construct of leadership.

Part IV (40 minutes)

1. Tell students that they are going to take inventory of their current skills in leadership using an inventory developed for high school students but with application to an older segment of the population as well. Not only will this inventory help them to reflect on their own level of leadership development, but it will also help them think about some of the elements and aspects of effective leadership that the class has not addressed.

2. Distribute copies of Handout 6.4: Leadership Self-Assessment Inventory. Briefly walk students through the pages to see if there are any questions. Point out that the first section is a profile that asks them to record and capture background information and ideas about variables that relate to leadership potential. The second section is a rating scale for specific skill sets associated with leading and managing. Students are not yet ready in their lives to fill out the very last piece of the rating scale that is targeted to practicing professionals, but they are encouraged to read that piece to see what skill sets are needed for moving beyond mastery in a number of fields. Give students about 30 minutes to complete the inventory. If they need more time, encourage them to take it home with them, but be sure their completed forms are included in their portfolios.

3. Debrief the exercise by asking some students to share their responses on the items requiring them to develop futuristic scenarios. These scenarios go out 5 and 10 years. Ask them to think about themselves at age 40 and ask them what they will be doing then. Keep this discussion light-hearted.

4. Wrap up this part of the lesson by asking them what they learned, if anything, from completing and discussing the inventory. Point out that the Leadership Self-Assessment Inventory will serve as their journal entry for this lesson. If they did not get the inventory completed, they should use out-of-class time to finalize their responses. Remind them that the next leader to be studied is Maya Lin.

Assessment

Use the student responses to Handout 6.2 as the assessment for this lesson. Record your assessments in your gradebook before returning the completed handouts to students. Be sure Handout 6.4 is inserted into student portfolios.

Homework

The homework for the next lesson has already been assigned. There is no additional homework unless students need to put more time into completing Handout 6.4.

Extensions

There are no extensions for this unit.

List of Suggested Differences Between Managers and Leaders

Source	Managers	Leaders
The 108 Skills of Natural Born Leaders (Warren Blank)	• Influence derives from formal authority. • Authority invests them with the right to command and demand, require, and force compliance. • Authority can only be used down the organizational ladder.	• Influence derives from the quality of the interaction with followers. • Influence comes from commitment and passion and the ability to persuade others. • Influence can be exerted in any direction: up, across, down, and outside.

Learning to Lead (Warren Bennis and Joan Goldsmith)	• Managers:
	  – administer and maintain,
	  – accept reality and the status quo,
	  – rely on controls,
	  – have a short-range view,
	  – ask how and when, and
	  – focus on the bottom line.
		• Leaders:
		  – develop and innovate,
		  – investigate and challenge reality,
		  – inspire trust,
		  – have a long-range view,
		  – ask what and why, and
		  – focus on the horizon.

The Leadership Training Activity Book (Lois Hart and Charlotte Waisman)	• Managers:
	  – do things correctly,
	  – plan tactics,
	  – rely on analytical decision-making skills,
	  – are risk cautious,
	  – fear anarchy, and
	  – set standards of performance.
		• Leaders:
		  – do the correct thing,
		  – plan strategy,
		  – draw on intuitive insights and monitor gut feelings,
		  – take necessary risks,
		  – fear inertia, and
		  – set standards of excellence.

Name: _____ Date: _____

Leadership Generalizations Matrix

Instructions: Insert the names of three of the leaders who have been studied in this unit into the empty boxes in the first row. Then complete the subsequent rows for the three generalizations listed as each one is applied to the leaders you selected. You may add additional sheets of paper to record your thinking on these applications.

Generalization in Unit			
Leadership requires vision—the ability to see beyond what is to what might be by bridging the present and the future.			
Leadership is highly dependent on the interplay of intellectual abilities, specific aptitudes and skills, and personality factors.			
Leadership requires strong beliefs and core values and the passion and tenacity to act in accordance with them.			

Handout 6.3

Master Roster of Panel Questions

Key Idea or Issue	Specific Question and Any Follow-Up Components	Whole Panel or Specific Member	Student Responsible for Asking the Question

Leadership Self-Assessment Inventory

Name: _____ Date: _____ Age: _____

Part A. Multifactor Profile for High School Level

Family History and Birth Order Variables

What is your birth order in the family?

❑ Only child   ❑ Oldest child   ❑ Middle child   ❑ Youngest child

How do you think this has impacted your leadership role in your family?

List noteworthy leadership roles or traits in evidence in your family history (including parents, grandparents, and older siblings).

Name	Relationship	Role(s) or Trait(s)

Your Educational History

Level	School/Site	Relevant Comments or Notations
Elementary		
Middle or Junior High		
High School		
Summer Enrichment		
Special Lessons (Tutoring) and Area		

Describe your areas of academic strength.

Describe any academic awards or achievements you have accrued/attained to date (e.g., in upper percentile on PSAT or SAT, Academic Challenge participant, winner of essay contest for school, perfect attendance record holder).

Aptitudes and Special Interests

Describe any special interests, hobbies, or talents you have developed to date, including athletic/sports participation, band or choir membership, drama/dance/art activities, chess, and the like.

List any extracurricular organizations to which you belong, such as Boy or Girl Scouts of America, Big Brothers or Sisters, youth groups in your church or place of worship, and the like.

List any leadership roles you have assumed in any of your educational or extracurricular activities, such as class president or officer, organization president or officer, committee head, project manager, team captain, student council representative, lead chair in clarinet section, director of play, and the like.

Personality Characteristics

Using the following continua, put an X on the line that describes where you see yourself in relation to the personality trait or behavioral inclination.

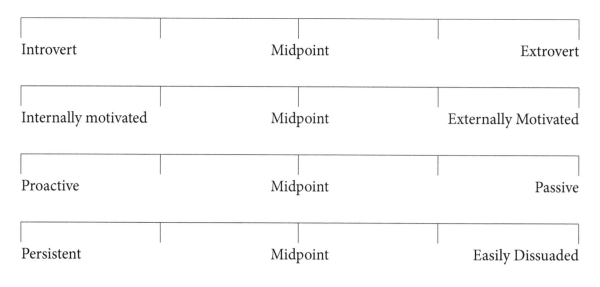

Introvert	Midpoint	Extrovert
Internally motivated	Midpoint	Externally Motivated
Proactive	Midpoint	Passive
Persistent	Midpoint	Easily Dissuaded

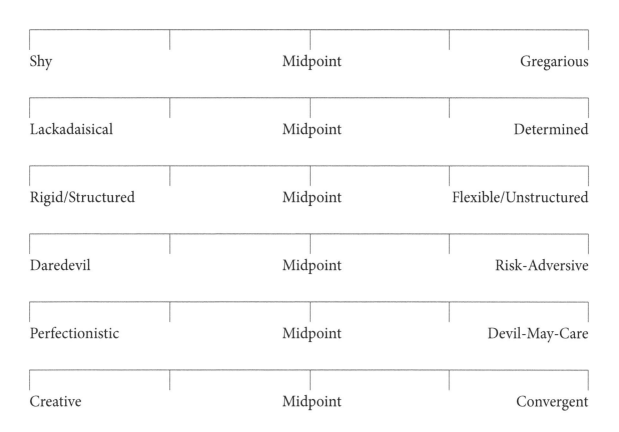

Shy | Midpoint | Gregarious

Lackadaisical | Midpoint | Determined

Rigid/Structured | Midpoint | Flexible/Unstructured

Daredevil | Midpoint | Risk-Adversive

Perfectionistic | Midpoint | Devil-May-Care

Creative | Midpoint | Convergent

Pick two of the factors where you are positioned toward the extreme left or right on the scale and give an example of your behavior in relation to those two factors. If you fall in the middle on every dimension, give an example drawn from two factors only.

Do you prefer to be in the spotlight or behind the scenes in team-oriented activities or projects?

Do you prefer to work alone, with one other person, or in small or large groups?

Are you self-directed or do you need prodding to get work/assignments completed on time?

Career Aspirations

At this juncture, in what field or specialization do you envision your future career?

What is the highest position you wish to attain in this career if you reach the threshold of success to which you aspire?

Is this consistent with the career you would most like to have if other factors were in play? If not, what career would you rather pursue/consider?

List at least two of your professional role models and explain why you have chosen them.

Values/Beliefs

Identify and list three beliefs you hold about the world, people, life in general, or other areas of philosophical inquiry that are important to you in defining who you are.

Identify and list three values that are important to you in defining who you are and/or who you aspire to be.

Identify at least two role models who exemplify or embody the beliefs and/or values you have cited and explain why you have chosen them. These may be the same as the role models you have cited in the section on career aspirations, but the reasons for choosing them in this category might be different.

Definition of Success

Where will you be and what will your life look like 5 years from now if you are successful in pursuing your career aspirations and living by the values and beliefs to which you hold or aspire? Create a brief scenario for this hypothetical situation.

Where will you be and what will your life look like 10 years from now if you are successful in pursuing your career aspirations and living by the values and beliefs to which you hold or aspire? Create a brief scenario for this hypothetical situation.

What is your definition of and metric (standard) for ultimate success in life?

To what extent does being a leader in your chosen career and/or avocation constitute an important component of your definition of success? Explain.

What academic shortcomings or personality characteristics do you have that might undermine your achievement of success?

How can you remediate, circumvent, or override these conditions so that you are able to maximize your potential for achieving success?

Part B. Leadership Skills Rating Scale

Directions: Using the following rating scale, place an X in the column that most accurately describes your developmental/mastery level for each of the skills specified:

NA = Not Applicable at This Time   1 = Minimal
2 = Developing (In Progress)   3 = Proficient   4 = Awesome

Categories and Skill Sets	NA	1	2	3	4
Visioning Skills					
• Can relate to and describe the big picture					
• Can conceptualize and articulate ideas/solutions					
• Can imagine how ideas or alternatives will play out if pursued					
• Can mentally synthesize disconnected/fragmented pieces into a unified whole					
• Can integrate ideas/insights from one field into another (cross-pollination)					
Motivational Skills					
• Can establish rapport through conversation and interpersonal interaction					
• Understands internal and external motivation and helps others access the feedback/rewards/supports most compatible with their own needs for success					
• Can convey optimism in facing challenges or setbacks					
• Can coach, mentor, and act as a role model in influencing the performance of others					
• Can recognize and acknowledge the contributions of others					
• Can implement celebratory events as warranted					
• Can tolerate missteps or noncatastrophic mistakes that allow others to grow					
• Can inspire through stewardship and humility					
Communication Skills					
• Can use empathic listening strategies					
• Can write clearly, cogently, and persuasively					
• Can prepare and deliver effective speeches					
• Can use storytelling to make points or share ideas					
• Can use technology and audio/visual aids to good advantage					
• Can adjust vocabulary, sentence construction, and degree of formality of message to suit intended receiver/audience					

Categories and Skill Sets	Rating				
	NA	1	2	3	4
Team-Building Skills					
• Values diversity and encourages independent thinking in others					
• Solicits input and involves others in decision making					
• Facilitates open communication among team members					
• Encourages team members to access learning and development opportunities					
• Allows for constructive conflict and diffuses destructive conflict					
• Gives positive feedback and addresses concerns/issues before serious problems emerge					
Conflict Resolution Skills					
• Understands that conflict is inevitable and can lead to improved performance or outcomes if managed appropriately					
• Has knowledge of and deploys appropriate conflict resolution style for situations encountered (direct, avoidance, accommodation, collaboration)					
• Promotes win-win resolutions					
Decision-Making Skills					
• Has knowledge of and deploys appropriate decision-making models as needed					
• Can calculate risks and weigh consequences					
• Allows for midcourse corrections in decisions made by identifying contingencies					
• Can accept responsibility for failure as well as for success					
• Understands that power and authority are derived through multiple channels and can identify the relevant channel in play					
Strategic Planning Skills					
• Can identify gaps and needs					
• Can clarify goals and help define objectives and outcomes					
• Can evaluate proposed action plans, timelines, people, and resource needs for likelihood of success or failure					
• Can articulate benchmarks to measure progress and ultimate success					

Categories and Skill Sets	Rating				
	NA	1	2	3	4
Managerial and Follow-Through Skills					
• Can delegate tasks appropriately					
• Can prioritize tasks based on importance and urgency					
• Can adhere to timelines or other commitments					
• Can deliver products or results with minimal supervision					
• Can secure necessary human and fiscal resources to get job done					
• Can remove people from tasks or roles as needed without compromising their dignity					
• Can hold self and others accountable					
Critical Thinking and Problem-Solving Skills					
• Can accurately define problems and can narrow or enlarge the scope of the problem to ensure accuracy of perception					
• Can use brainstorming to generate a variety of solutions					
• Can collect and analyze relevant information and data to verify perceptions					
• Can use logic and reasoning skills with dexterity; recognizes the role of intuition in guiding one's judgment regarding choices					
Advocacy and Public Relations Skills					
• Can demonstrate passion by combining competence, commitment, and enthusiasm					
• Can organize information and arguments to inform and to engender support for one's platform or agenda					
• Can identify relevant stakeholders and tailor information and delivery channels to their needs					
• Is visible at important events and appears engaged and focused at all times					
Domain Expertise Skills (for practitioners only)					
• Completes relevant training					
• Attains relevant degrees and/or certification/licensure					
• Engages in sufficient on-the-job training and/or task/role repetition to perform tasks effortlessly					
• Understands that domain-mastery builds credibility and trust					

Categories and Skill Sets	Rating				
	NA	1	2	3	4
Domain Expertise Skills, continued					
• Establishes connections to other professionals and leaders in the field					
• Stays abreast of knowledge, new research, and development in the field					
• Knows and abides by the ethics and standards of conduct of the field					
• Guards against one's own resistance to changes in practice but does not compromise one's integrity or values					
• Assumes responsibility for as needed and/or champions the contributions of the field beyond one's immediate role or part					

Lesson 7
Maya Lin and Creativity and Innovation

Sometimes I think creativity is magic; it's not a matter of finding an idea, but allowing the idea to find you.

—Maya Lin

Instructional Purpose

- To practice using the Internet to do biographical research
- To map biographical data against key leadership factors
- To examine and practice strategies for innovative and creative thinking

Materials Needed

- Handout 7.1: Biographical Chart: Maya Lin
- Handout 7.2: Types of Creative Solutions to Problems
- Handout 7.3: Skills That Distinguish Innovators
- Handout 7.4: Two Activities to Stimulate Creative Thinking
- Handout 7.5: Journal Entry Questions
- Teachers' Rap Sheet on Maya Lin (see Appendix A)

Activities and Instructional Strategies

Part I (1 period if homework has been completed)

1. In the homework assignment for Lesson 5, students were directed to the Internet to collect biographical data on Maya Lin, renowned contemporary architect and sculptor and ecological artist. Ask students if any of them have been to either the Vietnam Veterans Memorial in Washington, DC, or to any of her other memorials, installations, or exhibitions and discuss their reactions to them. If you have been to one or more of these sites, feel free to share your personal reaction as a way of connecting the class to the work of the artist. Ask students to calculate how old Maya Lin is today. This will orient them to her status as a contemporary leader. For alternatives to doing the research as homework or for doing only portions of the Biographical Chart, see Part I of Lesson 2.

2. Group students into groups of 4–5 and have them create master charts on Maya Lin using the information collected by each student. As they review their charts, advise them to add any important points that have not been

recorded but that they remember from reading the material. After allowing 30–35 minutes for this, ask the groups some questions that will ensure that they have retrieved some of the most salient information about Ms. Lin. Sample questions are as follows:

- Where did Lin grow up and how did her upbringing contribute to the direction she took in her career? What interesting tidbit did you discover about her family's immigration?
- What were some of her childhood interests?
- What achievement launched her career and how old was she at the time?
- What structural and/or environmental elements have been incorporated into her sculptural work?
- In complement to her art, what causes or issues has she advocated?
- What are some of the major awards she has received?
- What quotation of hers did you find the most interesting?

3. The teacher may choose to annotate the information collected by drawing on the Teachers' Rap Sheet for Ms. Lin if students have failed to grasp and/or record important pieces of biographical information.

4. Conclude this part of the lesson by asking: Who of the four previous leaders studied is Maya Lin most like and in what way? Who is she the most different from and in what way?

Part II (1 period)

1. The teacher will engage students in a large-group discussion using the following questions:
   - In what ways is Maya Lin a leader? Probe for justification if needed. In what way, if any, is leadership in the arts different from leadership in other fields of endeavor? What aspects does it have in common with other fields?
   - To what extent did time, place, and circumstances impact Lin's ability to become a leader?
   - How would you describe the vision that Maya Lin brings to the field of the visual arts? What kinds of problems or needs engage Lin's curiosity? What patterns or themes can you detect in her work? In what ways if any has her family's Asian heritage influenced her art?
   - What evidence is there of initiative, perseverance, and risk taking in Ms. Lin's profile? Can you think of any artists or scientists who achieved early success and recognition but were stymied by the experience (e.g.,

Harper Lee, Joseph Heller)? What do you think gave Lin the ability to risk failure after early national recognition and acclaim?

o What other personal characteristics contribute to Lin's success as a practicing artist? Was Lin a target of racism at any point in her life? What insights did you glean about how she handled such situations? In what ways, if any, has Lin demonstrated professional or personal growth or change over the course of her career?

o What do you see as Lin's lasting impact and contributions in the field of art? Have any of her works extended the envelope in architecture or sculpture? To what extent is her work innovative? What earlier architects or artists are you familiar with that Lin's work might evoke or pay homage to? One of her criteria for measuring the success of her work is "to give people a different way of looking at their surroundings; that's art to me." Do you think she has been successful in meeting this self-imposed standard? How so?

o Maya Lin said: "Every memorial in its time has a different goal." What did she mean by this and what is its relevance to the study of leadership? Think of some memorials that have been built in your lifetime (9/11 Memorial in New York City; National WWII Memorial and Martin Luther King, Jr. National Memorial in Washington, DC). What do you think the goals of these memorials are? Speculate as to how the passage of time will erode or enhance the connections that future generations will make to these memorials. (Note to teacher: If you have the technology available, project a photograph of any contemporary memorials for the students to look at while pondering this query.)

o Ask: If you had to create a painting or sculpture to represent Maya Lin's life, what image would you capture? What medium would you use? What artistic period or style would you draw on for inspiration? (Give students a few minutes to think about their answers for these questions.)

Part III (1 period)

1. Tell students that this part of the lesson deals with the fourth generalization on creativity and innovation. Ask them to define the word *innovation* and put some of their ideas on the board. Then ask students if the words *creativity* and *innovation* are synonymous. Prompt their responses so that they see that creativity is necessary but not sufficient for innovation. In other words, one can be creative, but the product of that creativity does not always result in an innovation unless it changes something beyond the individual. Writing a poem or painting a landscape are creative activi-

ties, but they do not rise to the level of innovation unless they change the boundaries of the medium or are recognized or adopted by others. Tell them that some theorists differentiate between creativity with a small "c" and creativity with a capital "C" that requires something to change. Howard Gardner, a Harvard psychologist, has stated that "the acid test of creativity is whether after a person does his or her thing they actually change the way other people see the world" (Salzberg, 2010, para. 1). He goes on to say that one cannot be creative unless one has mastered at least one discipline, art, or craft—and that takes about 10 years.

2. Distribute Handout 7.2: Types of Creative Solutions to Problems and review the information. Ask students to cite examples of innovations in the first three categories and give an example of a creative output that falls into the last category.

3. Tell students that there is a body of research that indicates people can be taught to be more creative in their thinking and doing. For instance, in an article entitled "The Innovator's DNA," Dyer, Gregersen, and Christensen (2009) examined the habits of 25 innovative entrepreneurs and found that the most innovative among them spent 50% more time on discovery-related activities than their least innovative counterparts. These researchers identified five skills that are associated with the creative mindset. Distribute Handout 7.3: Skills That Distinguish Innovators and briefly review it with students. After reviewing it, emphasize that in order to have a creative breakthrough that leads to significant change, one must have a level of knowledge of a given field that allows one to know what has already been done.

4. Break students into small groups and distribute Handout 7.4: Two Activities to Stimulate Creative Thinking. Tell students that they have 15 minutes to work on filling in the boxes on the first exercise, Frame the Name. Explain that their task is to brainstorm names or slogans for the items in Column 1 based on the categories in Columns 2–6. They should fill in as many boxes as they can within the time limit. An example of a response for the flying car with a military association would be the "paratroop coupe." Call time after the 15 minutes have elapsed, and then instruct them to complete the matrix in Activity 2, The "Eyes" Have It. Pick an object in the classroom such as the American flag or a map of the world. Have students put the name of the object in the box on the first line, and then have them fill in the subsequent boxes describing it through the lens of different roles or professions. An example of a flag seen through the eyes of an artist would be "a red, white, and blue star-studded banner." Call time after 10 minutes.

5. Debrief the exercise by having the small groups report the number of boxes they filled in within the time frame for the first activity. Then have each group share some of the ideas that the group is most proud of. Have the students nominate and vote for the best single answer for Frame the Name before debriefing the second activity, following a similar approach. Ask the following three questions to wrap up the exercise:

   o One of the ideas that Maya Lin expressed was: "Sometimes I think creativity is magic; it's not a matter of finding an idea, but allowing the idea to find you." What do you think she meant by this?

   o Did you have fun doing this part of the lesson? If yes, do you think there is any connection between play and creativity? Have them elaborate their answers.

   o Did any groups consider delegating sections of the task to individuals or subgroups in order to get more suggestions on the table? Why or why not?

Part IV (1 period or less)

1. Distribute Handout 7.5: Journal Entry Questions to students and allow them 15–20 minutes to select at least two and complete their journal entries. As an option, you may assign specific questions to individuals or to the whole class.

2. After the time has elapsed, ask for some volunteers to share their responses and discuss the questions as a whole class.

3. This part may also be done as homework as long as there is sufficient time between this class and the next one for the next biographical research to be completed.

Assessment

The teacher should check to see that each student has completed the Biographical Chart on Maya Lin and prepared written responses for the journal entry. Have students insert their own copies of the Handout 7.4 into their portfolios.

Homework

Students are assigned responsibility for completing Handout 8.1: Biographical Chart: Nikola Tesla in preparation for the next class period. The four sites that students should be directed to for conducting this research are as follows:

   ◎ Wikipedia (http://en.wikipedia.org/wiki/Nikola_Tesla)
   ◎ Tesla Memorial Society of New York (http://www.teslasociety.com)

◎ Tesla—Master of Lightning (http://www.pbs.org/tesla/)
◎ BrainyQuote (http://www.brainyquote.com/quotes/authors/n/nikola_tesla.html)

Extensions

The following ideas are offered as substitutions for parts of the above lesson or as extensions for this lesson focusing on Maya Lin and the role of creativity and innovation in leadership.

◎ In describing her book *Boundaries*, Lin made the following observation:

> *Boundaries* is about opposites. It's a contradiction. Everyone looks at boundaries as a division, and what I'm after is the boundary line—the space between two things. I see myself existing on the boundary line, and it's that line that begins to take on dimensionality. I feel I exist on the boundary somewhere between science and art, art and architecture, public and private, east and west. I'm always trying to find a balance between opposing forces. (Fry, 2000, para. 14)

Write the quotation on the board or give students a copy of it, then have them do the following:

○ Write a paper first explicating this idea and then applying it to yourself. What are the dualities that define and shape your identity and self-image? How does this sense of duality impact where you are now in your life and where you see yourself in the future?

○ Pen a diamante antonym poem capturing one of the dualities you have explored in your paper.

The above can be done as an either/or activity. For instructions on diamante poems, see the ReadWriteThink website (http://www.readwritethink.org).

◎ Have students investigate the Maya Lin Studio website (http://mayalin.com). It is a virtual reality art exhibition, almost devoid of text. Using the viewing as a stimulus, have them create an art object of their own. Options might include a collection of photographs; a collage; a literary piece such as a poem, a reflection, or a story; a musical composition such as a rap, a song, or a lullaby; a visual art piece such as a watercolor, a ceramic, or a tapestry; and so forth. Give wide latitude to the kind of artistic expression they prefer to pursue. Have them share the results with the class at a future session. Discuss the ideas and feelings that were engendered by the viewing and were catalyzed in the subsequent creative output. (This requires time in and out of class to complete.)

◎ Have students view the video on YouTube called "What Is Missing" (http://www.youtube.com/watch?v=K8NSt0k_KM4) filmed at the California Academy of Sciences in San Francisco to hear Lin discuss one of her more recent art pieces. They should watch the opening ceremony, but then advance the video to 31:15 to hear Lin discuss her ideas for this memorial (about 5 minutes of the program). The title piece focuses on the theme of the extinction of animals on our planet. Have students write a critique for the local paper or a blog site of the work. Have them conclude the critique with observations about Lin's leadership abilities as reflected in her more recent contributions (i.e., has she grown or diminished in her leadership role and skill set?). Ask that students not search for other accessible critiques or reports of the opening, but explore their own ideas and reactions.

Handout 7.1

Biographical Chart: Maya Lin

Full Name: _____

Lifespan: _____

Early Family Background and Created Family Structure

_____

_____

_____

Personality Characteristics and Areas of Aptitude, Talent, and Interest

_____

_____

_____

Major Career/Professional Events and Accomplishments

_____

_____

_____

Personal Life Themes/Beliefs

_____

_____

_____

Selected Quotations

_____

_____

_____

Awards and Recognition

_____

_____

_____

_____

Handout 7.2
Types of Creative Solutions to Problems
(Adapted from *Disciplined Dreaming* by Josh Linkner)

Breakthrough Innovations or Discoveries: Game changers that rewrite rules and shift paradigms; these solutions often create new platforms that initiate, spur, or support a cascade of subsequent developments or changes.

High-Value Innovations or Discoveries: Solutions that make significant improvements in systems, processes, or products that yield tangible value but do not dismantle or challenge the underlying theoretical or propositional base.

Incremental Innovations: Small changes or refinements that tinker with a component or aspect of a system, process, or product but contribute to the efficiency or effectiveness of it.

Noninnovative, but Novel or Unique Output: Products or ideas that reflect personal creativity but engender no change in thinking or behavior beyond that of the creator.

Handout 7.3
Skills That Distinguish Innovators
(Adapted from "The Innovator's DNA" by Jeffrey H. Dyer,
Hal B. Gregersen, and Clayton M. Christensen)

Associating: The ability to create links between seemingly unrelated items; sometimes referred to as analogical or metaphorical thinking.

Questioning: The ability to explore ideas and options without foreclosing on preconceived notions, assumptions, or patterns. Common questions such as Why?, Why not?, and What if? unshackle accepted and ingrained avenues of thought and challenge the status quo.

Observing: The ability to focus awareness (telescope) and to eliminate biases or distortions that contaminate how you see things (fresh eyes).

Experimenting: The ability and the persistence to try out multiple ideas, proposals, or solutions without fear of failure and to create a culture where others also feel safe in doing so. (One of the most effective experiments undertaken by innovators was living and working in a foreign country during part of their careers.)

Networking: The ability to expand the envelope of your thinking by seeking out diverse and divergent perspectives, including a willingness to be challenged.

Handout 7.4

Two Activities to Stimulate Creative Thinking

Activity 1: Frame the Name

Create a product name or slogan for the objects in the first column, drawing upon references or associations from Columns 2–6.

Object	Greek and Roman Mythology	Military Operations and Jargon	Romance and Sensuality	Harlem Renaissance and/ or Prohibition	Popular Films and Novels
Fluorescent nail polish color					
Dual passenger flying car					
Grid system for routing flying cars					
Snack food made from seaweed					
Wafer that eliminates sugar cravings					
Athletic shoes with trampoline soles					
Ad campaign to dissuade littering					
Your choice:					

Activity 2: The "Eyes" Have It

Pick an object in the classroom. Describe the object below through the eyes of the person in the first column.

Person	Object:
Visual Artist	
Politician	
Philosopher	
Scientist	
Historian	
Wizard	
Poet	
Soldier	

Handout 7.5
Journal Entry Questions

1. What did you learn from the biographical study of Maya Lin that is particularly illuminating in your understanding of leadership? In what ways is Lin a role model for you and other emerging leaders?

2. When Lin's design was selected for the Vietnam Veterans Memorial, there was some backlash because of her Asian heritage. What parallels can you draw between Lin and Marshall in terms of their responses to incidents of racism? What differences are worth noting? In today's society, what racial, ethnic, or other minority group do you think is most likely to face discrimination and why?

3. Maya Lin's middle name is Ying, which means "precious stone." In her book entitled *Boundaries*, she said: "My work is in part trying to mimic natural formations in the earth, complex but seemingly very simple." Cogitate on these two separate observations and let them lead you to some thoughts of your own on Lin's life and legacy.

4. How do you assess your own capacity for creativity? There is a body of research that suggests that in order to have breakthrough levels of creativity, three factors must come into play: individual abilities (intellectual and psychological), a domain in which the individual achieves mastery, and linkage to a field (other practicing professionals or opinion makers) that recognizes and disseminates the products of that creativity. What implications does this research have for helping people to develop and maximize their creative potential?

Lesson 8
Nikola Tesla and Legacy

Let the future tell the truth, and evaluate each one according to his work and accomplishments. The present is theirs; the future, for which I have really worked, is mine.

—Nikola Tesla

Instructional Purpose

- ◎ To practice using the Internet to do biographical research
- ◎ To map biographical data against key leadership factors
- ◎ To examine and reflect upon how time and history impact legacy in leadership

Materials Needed

- ◎ Handout 8.1: Biographical Chart: Nikola Tesla
- ◎ Handout 8.2: Four Frames of Leadership
- ◎ Handout 8.3: Five Ideas to Consider in Shaping One's Legacy
- ◎ Handout 8.4: Journal Entry Questions
- ◎ Teachers' Rap Sheet on Nikola Tesla (see Appendix A)

Activities and Instructional Strategies

Part I (1 period if homework has been completed)

1. In the homework assignment for the previous lesson, students were directed to the Internet to collect biographical data on Nikola Tesla, scientific genius and inventor extraordinaire. Ask students to calculate how old Tesla was at the turn of the century (1900). The answer is 44, which was the middle of his life span. Ask them to describe what the United States was like in 1900 in terms of some key variables such as where most people lived, how they got around, what inventions existed at the time, and what inventions were on the horizon. For alternatives to doing the research as homework or for doing only portions of the Biographical Chart, see Part I of Lesson 2.

2. Have the whole class complete a master Biographical Chart by using a white board or overhead projector to compile the information gathered by students. The teacher should start by asking: What did you discover about Dr. Tesla's early family background and created family structure? What did you discover about his education? Follow this format until

the master chart has been completed enough to ensure that the students have a fairly in-depth profile of the individual. The teacher may choose to annotate or extend the information in the Biographical Chart by drawing on the data provided in the Teachers' Rap Sheet found in Appendix A. Students should embellish their own charts as the class session unfolds.

3. Conclude this part of the lesson by pointing out that the farther we go back in time to study important people, the more difficult it is to relate to the context and culture in which they lived but the easier it is to understand the extent and importance of their contributions. Ask students if they think the passage of time has helped Tesla's legacy or diminished it.

Part II (1 period)

1. The teacher will engage students in a large-group discussion, using the following questions:

   o In what ways was Nikola Tesla a leader? Probe for justification, if needed. In what ways is leadership in the sciences the same as and different from leadership in the arts? What about in other applied fields such as business, politics, and the judiciary?

   o To what extent did time, place, and circumstances impact his ability to become a leader?

   o How would you describe the vision that Nikola Tesla brought to the fields of science and engineering? What kinds of problems engaged Tesla's curiosity? What ideas about religion, science, and humankind did he hold? How did he see his approach to problem solving as different from Edison's?

   o What evidence is there of initiative, perseverance, and risk taking in Dr. Tesla's profile?

   o What other personal characteristics contributed to Tesla's success as a scientist and engineer? Did any personal characteristics or conditions interfere with his getting the recognition and acclaim he may have deserved? In what ways, if any, did Tesla evidence personal growth or change over the course of his life?

   o What do you see as Tesla's lasting impact and contributions in the fields of science and engineering? Which of his inventions had the greatest impact on the world we live in today and why? What other inventors rival Tesla in the number and magnitude of their contributions in their respective time periods? How were Tesla and Jobs similar in regards to their professional contributions? How were they different?

   o Nikola Tesla said:

The practical success of an idea, irrespective of its inherent merit, is dependent on the attitude of the contemporaries. If timely, it is quickly adopted; if not, it is apt to fare like a sprout lured out of the ground by warm sunshine, only to be injured and retarded in its growth by the succeeding frost.

What did he mean by this and what is its relevance to the study of leadership? Can you cite an example of an idea that was launched before the world could grasp and appreciate it? What poetic device is embedded in Tesla's insight?

o If you were asked to create a mathematical equation to represent Nikola Tesla's life, how would you express it? (Give students a few minutes to think about their answers to this question.)

Part III (1 period)

1. Tell students that this part of the lesson deals with the fifth generalization that notes that leadership is judged through the lens of time and history. Ask students to define the word *legacy* and put some of their ideas on the board. (Dictionary definitions include money or property bequeathed in a will, something handed down from an ancestor or predecessor, and something that exists after death or from the past.) Then ask them to define the word through the eyes of (a) an artist like Lin (e.g., a legacy is the cornerstone of a monument to a person's life; a legacy is the beauty that transcends the temporality of a single existence) and (b) an inventor like Tesla (e.g., a legacy is a commitment to the future seen in hindsight; a legacy is a patent for the future). These questions are designed to bridge Lesson 7 on creativity with this lesson on legacy. There are no right or wrong answers.

2. Distribute Handout 8.2: Four Frames of Leadership and deliver a mini-lecture highlighting the following material:

   o In Lesson 6, we talked about basic management theory; managers are responsible for overseeing two elements: people and tasks. Lee Bolman and Terrence Deal (2006) proposed a leadership model that suggested that there are four frames by which leadership should be understood. They called the people element the *human relations frame* and the task element the *structural frame*.

   o They added two additional frames to the equation: the *political frame* deals with the distribution of power—the recognition that there are never enough resources to meet all needs so a leader must know how to fight for the right course of action and use conflict to promote personal and organizational growth in a healthy way. The fourth frame is the *symbolic frame*. This is the lens that draws on intuition as well as analysis to understand and resolve problems, to bring imagination and creativity to the leader's way. This is the lens that plies the tools of the artist's trade: the use of storytelling, icons, legends, and logos to shape ideas and the creation of rites and ceremonies to celebrate accomplishments. The master of the power-based lens is described as a "warrior" and the master of the symbolic lens is described as a "wizard."

o In their research on contemporary leaders in the business sphere, Bolman and Deal (2006) have found that more work needs to be done to prepare people to take on the mantles of warrior and wizard. Great leaders need the wizard's mastery of symbols and the warrior's mastery of power. They suggest that a leader's legacy is shaped by his or her ability to assume different roles at critical junctures in an organization's life cycle.

3. Ask if there are any questions at this point.
4. Break students into small groups and distribute Handout 8.3: Five Ideas to Consider in Shaping One's Legacy and tell students that these ideas came from Max De Pree, whose book, *Leading Without Power*, is about leadership in organizations that focus on nonpublic and charitable service and that primarily rely on volunteers instead of paid staff. De Pree (1997) defined legacy as "the cumulative informal record of how close we came to the person we intended to be" (p. 163). He noted that what you plan to do may differ enormously from what you leave behind. He advised that realizing our potential requires us to think purposefully about our legacy. Vision and legacy are like the bookends of each of our lives and for those of us who become leaders, these bookends take on more public dimensions. Have students discuss the elements using the questions at the bottom of the handout as their guide. Tell them to make notes on their discussion for inclusion in their portfolios.
5. Reconvene the whole class and debrief the discussion. Make a master list of any additional elements that students have articulated for consideration in shaping a legacy.

Part IV (1 period or less)

1. Distribute Handout 8.4: Journal Entry Questions to students and allow them 15–20 minutes to select at least two and complete their journal

entries. As an option, you may assign specific questions to individuals or to the whole class.

2. After the time has elapsed, ask for some volunteers to share their responses and discuss the questions as a whole class.

3. This part may also be done as homework or as an in-class small-group activity

Assessment

The teacher should check to see that each student has completed the Biographical Chart on Nikola Tesla, taken notes for the small-group discussion on legacy, and prepared a written response for the journal entry.

Homework

Students are reminded that the next lesson will involve the panel of leaders and to be thinking of any new questions they want to add as a result of studying Lin and Tesla, creativity, innovation, and legacy.

Extensions

The following ideas are offered as substitutions for parts of the above lesson or as extensions for this lesson focusing on Nikola Tesla and the impact of time and history on one's leadership legacy.

◎ Tesla and Westinghouse introduced the world to the advantages of the alternating current at the World Columbian Exposition in Chicago in 1893. Have students read the Wikipedia entry on this exposition, including the segment on Tesla's contribution (http://en.wikipedia.org/wiki/World's_Columbian_Exposition). Then have groups of students work together to develop the narrative for a 3–5-minute retrospective radio broadcast about the event to be aired at the 50-year anniversary (1943) of the exposition. (See if they make the connection that 1943 was the year Tesla died.)

◎ Have students watch the PBS documentary on Tesla entitled *Tesla: Master of Lightning* (about 1.5 hours). There is usually a DVD available through the local library, or a copy can be accessed through Netflix. If this is done as an in-class activity, have students discuss the following questions:

  ○ What did you learn about Tesla from watching the film that amplified and enriched your Internet research?

  ○ How effective was the film in selecting and showcasing the most important elements of Tesla's life and contributions?

- What, if anything, does studying Tesla teach us about leadership in science and engineering that differs from leadership in artistic domains?

◎ Have students read Tesla's autobiography *My Inventions: The Autobiography of Nikola Tesla* (which can be found on Amazon.com) and write a paper explicating three new ideas or insights that they took away from the text. Ask them if the benefit of hindsight (already knowing how history has judged Tesla) influenced how they viewed Tesla's self-revelations and in what way.

Biographical Chart: Nikola Tesla

Full Name: _____

Lifespan: _____

Early Family Background and Created Family Structure

_____

_____

_____

Personality Characteristics and Areas of Aptitude, Talent, and Interest

_____

_____

_____

Major Career/Professional Events and Accomplishments

_____

_____

_____

Personal Life Themes/Beliefs

_____

_____

_____

Selected Quotations

_____

_____

_____

Awards and Recognition

_____

_____

_____

_____

Handout 8.2

Four Frames of Leadership

Structural	Human Relations
Emphasis on Tasks Role: Architect	Emphasis on People Role: Catalyst
Political	**Symbolic**
Emphasis on Power Role: Warrior	Emphasis on Meaning Role: Wizard

Note. From Bolman and Deal (2006, 2008).

Handout 8.3

Five Ideas to Consider in Shaping One's Legacy

(From *Leading Without Power* by Max De Pree)

1. Truth is the first level of quality in a legacy.
2. Personal accountability is a foundation for a legacy.
3. A legacy sets standards.
4. Guiding legacies lift the spirit.
5. A legacy lives in the actions of many people.

Questions for Discussion

1. What does each element mean?

2. How important is each element in considering the idea of legacy?

3. Is a legacy in the arts shaped by different expectations or measured by different standards than a legacy in the sciences?

4. What relationship can one draw between innovation and legacy?

5. What are some of the different ways a society acknowledges or commemorates a legacy?

6. Can your group come up with three additional elements to consider in shaping one's legacy?

Handout 8.4

Journal Entry Questions for Tesla Lesson

1. What did you learn from the biographical study of Nikola Tesla that is particularly illuminating in your understanding of leadership? In what ways is Tesla a role model for you and other emerging leaders?

2. Tesla did not receive the recognition he deserved for his work on the radio until after his death, yet he once said: "I do not regret others having stolen my ideas. I do regret the fact that they do not have their own ideas." What can you infer regarding Tesla's values from this statement? Why do you think it took so long for Tesla to get the recognition he deserved for all of his contributions? Do you think he has the recognition he deserves today, or is he still overshadowed by native-born American inventors?

3. What relevance do the frames posited by Bolman and Deal have to the leadership skills exhibited by Nikola Tesla? Does he fit into one of the frames more so than the others, or does he show skills that apply to multiple frames? Explain or give an example to justify your answer. Where do you see your own skills or preferences as mapped against this model? That is, are you an architect of systems and tasks, a catalyst for deploying human resources (people), a warrior welding power and influence, and/or a wizard who creates symbols and messages to convey meaning?

4. Pretend that you have the gift of prescience, and you know you will live to be 100 years old. You are going to achieve all your dreams—although not necessarily in the way you had planned. In a nutshell, what will your obituary say about you? What will be your lasting legacy many years after your death?

Lesson 9
Local Panel of Leaders and Oral Debate

Instructional Purpose

- ◎ To provide real-world examples of leadership with whom students can discuss their ideas and insights
- ◎ To have students engage in a debate on a real-world issue related to the construct of leadership

Materials Needed

- ◎ Handout 6.3: Master Roster of Panel Questions
- ◎ Handout 9.1: Notes for Panel Discussion on Leadership
- ◎ Handout 9.2: Instructions for In-Class Debate
- ◎ Handout 9.3: Journal Entry Questions

Activities and Instructional Strategies

Part I (1 period)

1. Distribute to students a completed version of Handout 6.3: Master Roster of Panel Questions that you photocopied after Lesson 6 and Handout 9.1: Notes for Panel Discussion on Leadership and tell them to use it to record ideas that flow from the panel presentation. State that it is for their own use, and you will not be collecting it.

2. Introduce the panel to the class and ask each panel member to comment on his or her leadership role and to explain the organizational structure in which he or she operates. If he or she wants to, he or she may make a few observations about leadership as an opening statement, but this is optional. Tell panel members that the class has prepared a set of questions that they will be asked to respond to.

3. Facilitate the student questioning of the panel. At various junctures, ask students if they have any impromptu questions they would like to incorporate in the sequence. If students are not picking up on an important lead, model a question for them rather than letting the opportunity slide.

4. Provide a wrap-up to the panel discussion that summarizes a few important points made and point out a few similarities and differences among the perspectives of panelists. You are doing this to model listening and summarization skills to the students.

5. Thank the panel for coming, dismiss the panel participants, and ask for student volunteers to write thank-you notes to the panel (an individualized note to each panelist).

6. Debrief the panel discussion with students by asking the following questions:
   o What ideas did you find most intriguing from the panel members?
   o How has your interaction with the panel influenced your understanding of leadership?
   o What changes would you suggest if the next class were planning a panel discussion with leaders?

Part II (2–3 periods, depending on the size of the class)

1. Break students into groups of five to form debate teams. Assign each group a proposition to debate, either drawn from the following list or from ideas of your own:
   o Leadership should be taught as a separate unit to high school students rather than being integrated into the subject matter courses.
   o Leadership in the sciences has a more substantive impact on contemporary life and culture than leadership in the arts.
   o The Internet and globalization have profoundly changed the skill sets needed by leaders to succeed today.

   As an alternative, you may allow teams to select their own proposition, or you may assign team membership based on interest in a particular proposition.

2. Distribute Handout 9.2: Instructions for In-Class Debate and give students one class period to prepare their positions. If the class has too many teams, you may reduce the amount of time given to each role.

3. Hold the debate and have different students keep track of the time limits (rotate responsibility for this around the class).

4. After each group has debated, comment on the quality of the debate according to the following considerations: (a) organization, (b) clarity and balance in pro and con arguments, (c) ability of groups to develop reasonable arguments and to find or create evidence (such as student testimonials) to support their position, and (d) student composure in oral presentation.

5. Conclude this part of the lesson by asking students how practice in debate relates to the teaching of leadership skills.

Part III (30 minutes)

1. Distribute Handout 9.3: Journal Entry Questions to students and allow them 15–20 minutes to select at least two and complete their journal entries. As an option, you may assign specific questions to individuals or to the whole class.
2. After the time has elapsed, ask for some volunteers to share their responses and discuss the questions as a whole class.
3. Another option is to create small groups and assign each group two of the three questions, ensuring there is enough overlap so that all questions are covered but each group has a different combination.

Assessment

Have students insert Handout 6.3, their notes from the panel presentation, and their notes from the debate into their portfolios.

Homework

Remind students that their oral presentations will start in the next class session. If the presentations are likely to take more than one class period, tell students that they will be randomly assigned to a presentation order.

Extensions

◎ Have students select a local leader (not someone who is serving on the panel) to interview regarding leadership, contact the person, and schedule an interview. The interview may be done in person, on the phone, or online through e-mail or Skype. Have students prepare and submit a roster of questions to serve as the basis for the interview. Then have them conduct the interview, audiotape it or download the written responses, and write a summary (not a transcript) of the most interesting responses they got. Have them end their reports with their reflections about how the interview contributed to their understanding of leadership.

◎ Have students write a persuasive essay taking a position on a real-world issue, such as government bailouts of private industries or institutions, EPA regulations protecting endangered species, the government's role in the creation and expansion of alternative energies, term limits for Congressional seats, or regulation of information on the Internet. The structure of the essay must include three reasons with supporting evidence or documentation for the position and a rebuttal of three reasons against the position with supporting evidence or documentation. Have them conclude the essay by identifying what leadership role they can or would take to advance understanding or resolution of the issue.

Name: _____ Date: _____

Notes for Panel Discussion on Leadership

1. List the names and roles of panel members.

2. Identify points or ideas that you want to remember and who on the panel made them.

3. Jot down extemporaneous questions that come to mind that you want to ask.

Name: _____ Date: _____

Instructions for In-Class Debate

1. What is the proposition that your team has been assigned to debate?

2. Please assign roles in your group and structure your debate according to the following order and time limit:

   Student #1: Affirmative (5 minutes)

   Student #2: Negative (5 minutes)

   Student #3: Affirmative rebuttal (3 minutes)

   Student #4: Negative rebuttal (3 minutes)

   Student #5: Critique of the argument (5 minutes)

Handout 9.3
Journal Entry Questions

1. Reflect on what you learned about leadership from the panel discussion. What new ideas came to the forefront and what old ideas did you change or revise as a result of this experience? What did you observe about the panelists' ability to articulate information and to engage with an audience? What did the panelists do that established trust and built rapport with the group? How did you see yourself in the role of interacting with the panel? Were you an equal or were you intimidated by their age or authority?

2. Persuasive writing and oral debate both draw on reasoning abilities but require additional cognitive and affective skills to execute effectively. Discuss how you see these two skill sets. Where do they overlap? Where do they separate? Is one skill more important than the other for a leader? Which skill is strongest in you and which needs more development? Which of these skills will be of more utility in the profession you are planning to pursue?

3. What real-world problem or issue engages your interest and your commitment? Why are you invested in this problem? Will you be engaged with this problem or with solving it in the future (or are you an armchair advocate)? If you are to be so engaged, what role will you likely play? How will this unit on leadership help you in playing this role?

Lesson 10
Student Reports and Final Synthesis

Instructional Purpose

- ◎ To give students an opportunity to showcase their independent biographical research and their oral presentation skills
- ◎ To determine if students have internalized the dimensions of leadership studied (biographical elements and generalizations) in meeting their written report requirements
- ◎ To allow students to demonstrate their ability to synthesize leadership elements and ideas across leaders studied in the unit

Materials Needed

- ◎ Postassessment on the Concept of Leadership
- ◎ Teacher Template 10.1: Evaluation Form for Student Presentation
- ◎ Teacher Template 10.2: Evaluation Form for Written Report
- ◎ Handout 10.1: Peer Assessments of Oral Reports
- ◎ Handout 10.2: Journal Entry Questions

Activities and Instructional Strategies

Part I (1 or more periods, depending on the number of students in the class)

1. Distribute Handout 10.1: Peer Assessments of Oral Reports to students and explain that they will be critiquing the independent study presentations of their peers. Decide in advance if you want the reviews to be anonymous or not. Remind students that oral reports are to be limited to 7 minutes, and tell them that you will allow no more than three questions from the class per report.
2. Randomly assign students spots for their presentations, keep an eye on time limits, and facilitate the question and answer session following each presentation.
3. Ask each student a follow-up question tailored to his or her presentation that will give an opportunity to expand upon, defend, or rethink an important insight he or she acquired through the independent research project.

4. Complete Teacher Template 10.1: Evaluation Form for Student Presentation for each presentation as it finishes.

5. Collect peer assessment forms after each presentation. If you choose to, you should review the forms before giving them to the presenter. This is a good strategy for two reasons: (a) you never know what a student might put in writing to a peer, and (b) it will tell you if students have taken the critiquing role seriously or lightly.

6. Make some summary comments about the student presentations and tell the class you are looking forward to reading their written products. Use Teacher Template 10.2: Evaluation Form for Written Report to grade the students' papers.

Part II (1 period)

1. This part includes a culminating task for students. The teacher may choose to do it as an in-class writing assignment or as a small-group discussion, with either approach feeding into a large-group synthesis assignment. The decision for the strategy should be based on two factors: (a) the students' need for an additional in-class comprehensive writing task and (b) the level of energy left after the completion of oral and written reports.

2. The task is to develop a persuasive argument to either support or refute the eighth generalization in leadership addressed by the unit, drawing from the biographical studies done as a class and through independent study and any research-based information presented in the class to make one's case. This generalization is as follows: Leadership is grounded in knowledge of self and the belief in human agency to change the world. You may refer students to Handout 1.1 from the first unit lesson, or you may put the generalization on the board.

3. Advise students to defend their positions with at least three arguments in direct support and at least one argument that might dismantle a counter-case made by the opposition. This is an open-book assignment, and students may use their Biographical Charts, class notes, and journal entries as they see fit. Use most of the class period for student engagement in either writing or small-group discussion.

4. Depending on the approach taken to the assignment, allow some time for a whole-class synthesis. If done as a writing assignment, ask for volunteers to read one of the arguments that each of them crafted. If done as a small-group discussion, reconvene the whole group and ask each group to share one of the arguments that it delineated and polished.

5. Conclude the exercise by asking students if this generalization was harder or easier to defend or refute than the other generalizations they have studied and why.

Part III (20–30 minutes)

1. Distribute Handout 10.2: Journal Entry Questions to students and allow them 15–20 minutes to select at least two and complete their journal entries. As an option, you may assign specific questions to individuals or to the whole class.
2. After the time has elapsed, ask for some volunteers to share their responses and discuss the questions as a whole class.

Part IV (15–30 minutes)

1. One of the prevailing ideas in contemporary leadership theory was lightly touched upon in Lesson 8. This idea is that an element or strategy in leadership effectiveness is the creation or utilization of celebrations to mark important events. You can model this idea by having a small celebration of your students' accomplishments in completing this unit. You are encouraged to use your own creativity in designing this celebratory event.
2. Create certificates to give to students who demonstrated outstanding or unique performance in some way. For instance, you might give an award for best biographical presentation, best written report, best team player, best question raised, and so forth.
3. Invite the principal in to compliment the class on its hard work and to remind them that a successful school is one in which everyone pulls together to support academic success. Have the principal ask the students what they liked about the unit and what they would change. Model your willingness to be open to criticism as well as praise.

Part V (20 minutes)

1. Administer the postassessment found in the Pre- and Postassessments and Rubric section of this unit. If you are going to return the results to students, remember to give them their preassessment results at this time as well.

Assessment

When the written reports from Part I of this lesson are returned to students, these reports and their journal entries should be included in their portfolios. You may do the same with the pre- and postassessments and if Part II of this lesson was done as an individual writing assignment, this should also go into the portfolio. If grades are reported for the unit, use the student postassessment, student presentation and written report evaluation scores, student participation in group work, an assessment of the investment made in journal writing, and if appropriate, the individual writing assignment in Part II of this lesson as the basis for determining grades. Use the gain scores from the pre- and postassessments to document unit effectiveness.

Homework

Assign any work that leads the student into the next unit studied in your classroom or give them a free pass.

Extensions

There are no extensions for this lesson.

Evaluation Form for Student Presentation

Name of student:_____

Leader studied:_____ Date of presentation:_____

Please rate each student presentation using the following scale:

4 = Very Effective   3 = Effective   2 = Limited in its Effectiveness   1 = Ineffective

The presentation was thoughtful and well organized.	4	3	2	1
The presenter demonstrated a deep knowledge of his or her biographical subject.	4	3	2	1
The presentation followed the suggested format or made sound adjustments.	4	3	2	1
The presentation was creative.	4	3	2	1
The presenter engaged the audience effectively.	4	3	2	1

What was the best aspect of the presentation?

What could be improved next time?

Evaluation Form for Written Report

Name of student: _____

Title of paper: _____

Please rate the student paper on the self-selected biographical subject, using the following scale:

4 = Very Effective   3 = Effective   2 = Limited in its Effectiveness   1 = Ineffective

The paper is clear and well organized.	4	3	2	1
The paper is comprehensive in addressing the components required.	4	3	2	1
The paper integrates ideas about the leader with conceptions of leadership studied in the unit.	4	3	2	1
The paper offers insights about the leader's life with respect to his or her work and legacy.	4	3	2	1
The paper is mechanically competent with respect to grammar, usage, and spelling.	4	3	2	1

What are the strengths of the paper?

What are the areas of the paper that could be improved?

Name: _____ Date: _____

Peer Assessments of Oral Reports

Name of student presenting: _____ Leader studied:_____

Your name (if required by teacher): _____

Criteria	1 Low	2	3 Mid	4	5 High
Level of understanding of leader studied					
Evidence of both creativity and insight in doing assignment					
Ability to engage audience					

The best quality or element of this presentation was:

One idea for making it better next time is:

Handout 10.2
Journal Entry Questions

1. Of the leaders studied in this unit, who made the biggest impression on you and why? Who made the least impression on you and why? How judicious was the choice of these six leaders as the basis for unit development? Which leader would you have omitted and who would you have inserted in his or her place? What would be gained and what would be lost by your proposed alterations?

2. What aspect of leadership studied in this unit is most important for you to develop in yourself and why? How do you plan to go about strengthening your skill set in this area? How do you envision using this skill set in your future career or professional life? Is there an aspect of leadership this unit omitted that you want additional help with? How will you go about finding this help?

3. Develop three new generalizations about leadership that emerged from your biographical research across the six leaders you studied. Compare your three new generalizations to the eight generalizations studied in the unit in terms of their relative importance and ubiquity. In other words, would you recommend the unit be revamped based on any or all of your generalizations? Why or why not?

4. What growth do you see in yourself as a result of this unit of study? This may be academic growth or personal growth. Has anything changed in the way you think about leadership or in the way you currently behave as a leader or as a team player? Do you see the world any differently now? Give some detail or explication in your answer.

References

Bennis, W., & Goldsmith, J. (2010). *Learning to lead: A workbook on becoming a leader* (4th ed.). New York, NY: Basic Books.

Blank, W. (2001). *The 108 skills of natural born leaders*. New York, NY: Amacom.

Bolman, L. G., & Deal, T. E. (2006). *The wizard and the warrior: Leading with passion and power*. San Francisco, CA: Jossey-Bass.

Bolman, L. G., & Deal, T. E. (2008). *Reframing organizations: Artistry, choice, and leadership* (4th ed.). San Francisco, CA: Jossey-Bass.

Buckingham, M. (2005). *The one thing you need to know about great managing, great leading, and sustained individual success*. New York, NY: Free Press.

Cohen, W. A. (2008). *A class with Drucker: The lost lessons of the world's greatest management teacher*. New York, NY: Amacom.

Covey, S. R. (2004). *The 7 habits of highly effective people* (Rev. ed.). New York, NY: Simon and Schuster.

De Pree, M. (1997). *Leading without power: Finding hope in serving community*. San Francisco, CA: Jossey-Bass.

Dyer, J. H., Gregersen, H. B., & Christensen, C. M. (2009, December 21). The innovator's DNA. *Harvard Business Review*, 2–8.

Fry, P. (2000). *Maya Lin's Boundaries*. Retrieved from http://www.matilijapress. com/articles/mayalin.htm

Hart, L. B. & Waisman, C. S. (2005). *The leadership training activity book: 50 exercises for building effective leaders*. New York, NY: Amacom.

Kouzes, J. M., & Posner, B. Z. (1999). *The leadership challenge planner: An action guide to achieving your personal best*. San Francisco, CA: Jossey-Bass.

Li, C. (2010). *Open leadership: How social technology can transform the way you lead*. San Francisco, CA: Jossey-Bass.

Linkner, J. (2011). *Disciplined dreaming: A proven system to drive breakthrough creativity*. San Francisco, CA: Jossey-Bass.

Mai, R., & Akerson, A. (2003). *The leader as communicator: Strategies and tactics to build loyalty, focus effort, and spark creativity*. New York, NY: Amacom.

Maxwell, J. C. (2007). *Talent is never enough workbook*. Nashville, TN: Thomas Nelson.

National Association for Gifted Children. (2010). *NAGC Pre-K–Grade 12 Gifted Programming Standards: A blueprint for quality gifted education programs.* Washington, DC: Author.

National Governors Association Center for Best Practices, & Council of Chief State School Officers. (2010). *Common Core State Standards for English Language Arts.* Retrieved from http://www.corestandards.org/the-standards

Pappano, L. (2012). From math helper to community organizer: New longitudinal studies identify key factors in leadership development. *Harvard Educational Letter, 28*(1). Retrieved from http://www.hepg.org/hel/article/524#home

Partnership for 21st Century Skills. (2011). *Overview.* Retrieved from http://www.p21.org/overview/skills-framework

Payne, V. (2001). *The team-building workshop.* New York, NY: Amacom.

Quick, T. L. (1992). *Successful team building.* New York, NY: Amacom.

Salzberg, C. (2010). *Howard Gardner appeals to the creative mind.* Retrieved from http://www.fredonialeader.com/news/howard-gardner-appeals-to-the-creative-mind-1.1640823#.UFnQLkJwYc4

Taba, H. (1962). *Curriculum development: Theory and practice.* New York, NY: Harcourt, Brace.

Tushnet, M. V. (2001). *Thurgood Marshall: His speeches, writings, arguments, opinions, and reminiscences.* Chicago, IL: Lawrence Hill.

Williams, J. (2000). *Thurgood Marshall: American revolutionary.* New York, NY: Three Rivers Press.

Part IV
Appendices

Appendix A
Teachers' Rap Sheets

Teachers' Rap Sheet

Oprah Winfrey

Full Name: Oprah Gail Winfrey

Life Span: January 29, 1954 to Present

Early Family Background and Created Family Structure

- Born in Kosciusko, MS to an unmarried teenager, Vernita Lee, and Vernon Winfrey
- Mother was a housemaid; father was a barber and businessman
- Originally named Orpah after the biblical character in the book of Ruth
- Raised by grandmother, Hatti Mae Lee, until age 6
- Taught to read and write before age of 3
- Wore dresses made of potato sacks; received her first pair of shoes at age 6
- Moved to her mother's in Milwaukee, WI, when her grandmother became ill
- Three siblings: two half-sisters both named Patricia (one died of cocaine addiction) and one half-brother, Jeffrey, who died of AIDS
- Was raped at age 9 and endured years of sexual abuse from a cousin, uncle, and mother's boyfriend
- Became pregnant at 14; son died shortly after birth
- Moved to Nashville, TN, to live with her father and stepmother—home life very strict with church and education as the main focus
- 1992: Became engaged to Stedman Graham, a public relations executive; they have never married, but remained committed to each other

Education

- 1971: Graduated from East Nashville High School in Nashville, TN
- 1971–1976: Attended Tennessee State University
- 1987: Received a B.A. in speech and performing arts from Tennessee State University

Personality Characteristics and Areas of Aptitude, Talent, and Interest

- Has a positive sense of herself because of her grandmother's influence
- Has a passion for learning and gaining knowledge
- Her favorite book is *To Kill A Mockingbird* by Harper Lee
- Has shown ability to overcome adversity

- Skipped kindergarten after writing the teacher a note that she should be in first grade; the following year, she was promoted to third grade, skipping second
- Loved playing with farm animals as a child
- During high school she was a member of several clubs, including drama, debate, and student council
- Became an honors student during high school, was voted most popular girl, and was elected class president
- As a member of school speech team, placed second in the nation in dramatic interpretation
- Won Elks Club oratorical contest, receiving a full scholarship to Tennessee State University
- Invited to the White House Conference on Youth
- Enjoyed pageants and was crowned Miss Fire Prevention by WVOL, Miss Black Nashville, and Miss Black Tennessee
- Is an independent woman who is generous and influential
- Has an outgoing and empathetic personality
- Particular interest in women's and children's issues and education

Major Career/Professional Events and Accomplishments

- Began broadcasting career at WVOL radio in Nashville while still in high school
- Became youngest person (age 19) and Nashville's first African American female to coanchor the evening news at WTVF-TV
- Coanchored Baltimore's WJZ-TV *Six O'Clock News*; while there, also cohosted its local talk show, *People Are Talking*
- 1984: Hosted *AM Chicago*, making it number one local talk show, surpassing ratings for *The Phil Donahue Show*
- 1984: Show was renamed *The Oprah Winfrey Show*
- 1985: Costarred in Steven Spielberg's movie, *The Color Purple*
- 1986: *The Oprah Winfrey Show* entered national syndication, becoming the highest-rated talk show in television history
- 1988: Established Harpo Studios, which made her the third woman in American entertainment industry to own her own studio
- 1989: Produced and costarred in the drama miniseries *The Women of Brewster Place*
- 1989: Cofounded the women's cable television network *Oxygen*
- 1991: Proposed federal child protection legislation designed to keep nationwide records on convicted child abusers; pursued a ruling that would guarantee strict sentencing of individuals convicted of child abuse (Oprah Bill signed by President Clinton)

- 1993: Hosted a rare prime-time interview with Michael Jackson, which became the fourth most watched event in American television history and the most watched interview ever, having an audience of 36.5 million viewers
- 1996: Introduced the Oprah's Book Club segment on her television show
- 1997: Created the Oprah.com website to provide resources and interactive content related to her shows, magazines, book club, and public charity
- 2000: *O, The Oprah Magazine* launched with circulation of 500,000; had increased its readership to 2.65 million 3 years later
- 2006: Announced a 3-year, $55 million contract with XM Satellite Radio, establishing a new radio channel
- 2008: Harpo Films signed exclusive deal to develop and produce scripted series, documentaries, and movies for HBO
- Voiced Gussie, the goose for *Charlotte's Web* (2006); voiced Judge Bumbleton in *Bee Movie* (2007); voiced Eudora in *The Princess and the Frog* (2009); and narrated U.S. version of BBC nature program *Life* for the Discovery Channel
- 2008: Announced plans to change Discovery Health Channel into a new channel called OWN: Oprah Winfrey Network; launch delayed until January 2011
- 2006: To celebrate two decades on national TV, took her staff and their families (1,065 people in total) on vacation to Hawaii
- 2011: Series finale of *The Oprah Winfrey Show* aired on May 25
- Has coauthored five books
- 1985–2012: Has been in 18 films
- 1989–2012: Has directed 27 movies, TV series, and documentaries
- Has been ranked the highest-paid performer on television, the richest self-made woman in America, the richest African American of the 20th century, the greatest Black philanthropist in American history, and was for a time the world's only Black billionaire

Personal Life Themes/Beliefs

- Grandmother, father, and fourth-grade teacher were the most influential people in her life
- Church was an important part of life growing up
- Approaches her life and work with reverence and gratitude
- Strong belief in empowerment; people can change their lives for the better

Selected Quotations

◎ "As you become more clear about who you really are, you'll be better able to decide what is best for you—the first time around."

◎ "Be thankful for what you have; you'll end up having more. If you concentrate on what you don't have, you will never, ever have enough."

◎ "Biology is the least of what makes someone a mother."

◎ "Books were my pass to personal freedom. I learned to read at age three, and soon discovered there was a whole world to conquer that went beyond our farm in Mississippi."

◎ "Breathe. Let go. And remind yourself that this very moment is the only one you know you have for sure."

◎ "Do the one thing you think you cannot do. Fail at it. Try again. Do better the second time. The only people who never tumble are those who never mount the high wire. This is your moment. Own it."

◎ "Doing the best at this moment puts you in the best place for the next moment."

◎ "Excellence is the best deterrent to racism or sexism."

◎ "Follow your instincts. That's where true wisdom manifests itself."

◎ "For every one of us that succeeds, it's because there's somebody there to show you the way out."

◎ "My philosophy is that not only are you responsible for your life, but doing the best at this moment puts you in the best place for the next moment."

◎ "Before you agree to do anything that might add even the smallest amount of stress to your life, ask yourself: What is my truest intention? Give yourself time to let a yes resound within you. When it's right, I guarantee that your entire body will feel it."

◎ "Real integrity is doing the right thing, knowing that nobody's going to know whether you did it or not."

◎ "Getting my lifelong weight struggle under control has come from a process of treating myself as well as I treat others in every way."

◎ "Use what you have to run toward your best—that's how I now live my life."

◎ "Whatever you fear most has no power—it is your fear that has the power."

◎ "What I know for sure is that what you give comes back to you."

Awards and Recognition

◎ 1986: Academy Award and Golden Globe Nominations for Best Supporting Actress for *The Color Purple*

◎ 1989; 1993–1995: Received NAACP Image Award

◎ 1999: Named NAACP Entertainer of the Year

- 1995: Received Individual Achievement Award (George Foster Peabody Awards)
- 1996: Received Gold Medal Award from the International Radio & Television Society Foundation
- 1997: Named *Newsweek*'s Most Important Person in Books and Media
- 1997: Named *TV Guide*'s Television Performer of the Year
- 1998: Received Lifetime Achievement Award from the National Academy of Television Arts & Science
- Received more than 40 Daytime Emmy Awards®: seven for Outstanding Host, nine for Outstanding Talk Show, and more than 20 in the Creative Arts categories
- 1999: Received National Book Foundation's 50th Anniversary Gold Medal
- 1999: Received Black Film Award Nomination for Best Actress for *Beloved*
- 1999: Named PGA Producer of the Year for *Tuesdays With Morrie*
- 2000: Received Primetime Emmy Outstanding Made for Television Movie for *Tuesday With Morrie*
- 2002: Received Bob Hope Humanitarian Award
- 2003: Received Association of American Publishers Honors Award
- 2004: Received United Nations Association of the United States of America Global Humanitarian Action Award
- 2005: Received International Emmy Founders Award
- 2007: Received Elie Wiesel Foundation Humanitarian Award
- 2010: Received Minerva Award
- 2011: Received Jean Hersholt Humanitarian Award/Honorary Academy Award
- 2004–2011: Been included in eight of *TIME Magazine*'s 100 Most Influential People in the World lists

Lasting Impact and Contributions

- Best known as a media proprietor, talk show host, actress, producer, and philanthropist
- Her self-titled, multi-award-winning talk show became the highest-rated program of its kind in TV history
- Considered one of the most influential women in the world and has had a profound influence over the way people around the world read, eat, exercise, feel, and think about themselves and the world around them
- One of the wealthiest women in America, and one of the most generous both nationally and internationally

Teachers' Rap Sheet
Steve Jobs

Full Name: Steven Paul Jobs

Life Span: February 24, 1955–October 5, 2011

Early Family Background and Created Family Structure

- Born in San Francisco, CA, to two university students, Joanne Carole Schieble and Syrian-born Abdulfattah "John" Jandali, who were unmarried at the time
- Was adopted at birth by Paul Reinhold Jobs and Clara Jobs
- Unknown to him, his biological parents would later marry, have a second child, Mona Simpson, in 1957, and divorce in 1962
- Stated in authorized biography that Paul and Clara Jobs "were my parents 1,000%"
- Father was a machinist for a company that made lasers; mother was an accountant for Varian Associates, one of the first high-tech firms in what became known as Silicon Valley
- Jobs family moved to Mountain View, CA, when Steve was 5 years old
- Parents adopted another baby, a daughter named Patti
- Learn to read before beginning school
- Was taught rudimentary electronics by his father
- Saw first computer at age 12
- While in high school, attended lectures at the Hewlett-Packard plant; was offered a summer internship with Hewlett-Packard
- Enrolled in the Hewlett-Packard Explorer Club
- 1978: Birth of first child, Lisa Brennan-Jobs, with longtime partner Chris Ann Brennan; denied paternity, but later acknowledged daughter
- 1991 married Laurene Powell
- Had one son and two daughters
- Family lives in Palo Alto, CA

Education

- 1972: Graduated from Homestead High School in Cupertino, CA
- 1972: Attended Reed College in Portland, OR; dropped out after 6 months and spent next 18 months auditing creative classes
- 1974: Studied Eastern religions in India

Personality Characteristics and Areas of Aptitude, Talent, and Interest

- Was a prankster whose fourth-grade teacher needed to bribe him to study
- Tested so well in school, administrators wanted to skip him ahead to high school—a proposal his parents declined
- Swam competitively
- As a young boy, interested in electronics and gadgetry (technical tinkering)
- Member of Homebrew Computer Club
- An intelligent and innovative thinker; his biographer Isaacson said he had imaginative leaps that were instinctive and at times magical
- Strong ability to focus and preferred simplicity
- Perfectionistic
- Exhibited very demanding and aggressive behavior; at times was even nasty
- Had uncanny ability to convince himself and others to believe almost anything

Major Career/Professional Events and Accomplishments

- Early 1970s: Jobs and friend Steve Wozniak designed and illegally sold "blue boxes" that generated necessary tones to manipulate the telephone network, allowing free long-distance calls
- 1974: Created a circuit board for Atari's arcade video game Breakout
- 1976; Jobs, Wozniak, and Ronald Wayne founded Apple Computer, Inc. in Jobs's parents' garage
- First creation was the Apple I—the guts of a computer without a case, keyboard, or monitor; started by selling circuit boards, but later produced a complete computer prototype
- 1977: Apple II hit the market; became so popular Apple Computer, Inc. goes public, making Jobs's net worth $200 million by age 25
- Was among first to see the commercial potential of Xerox PARC's mouse-driven graphical user interface, which led to the creation of the Apple Lisa and Macintosh
- 1985: Forced out of Apple
- Started a company, NeXT, that built workstation computers; the world's first web browser was created on the NeXT computer; computer was the basis for today's Macintosh OS X and iPhone operating system (iOS)
- 1986: Jobs purchased The Graphics Group (later renamed Pixar Animation Studios), which specialized in computer animation from filmmaker George Lucas; the company has produced box-office hits such as *Toy Story, A Bug's Life, Toy Story 2, Monster's Inc., Finding Nemo, The Incredibles, Cars, Ratatouille, WALL-E, Up,* and *Toy Story 3*

◎ 2006: Sold Pixar to The Walt Disney Co. for $7.4 billion in stock
◎ 1991: Appointed to the President's Export Council
◎ 1996: Announcement that Apple Computer, Inc. would buy NeXT for $427 million, bringing Jobs back to the company he cofounded.
◎ Under Jobs's guidance, Apple increased sales significantly with the introduction of the iMac and other new products, appealing designs, and powerful branding
◎ 2010: Unveils the iPad, "the biggest thing Apple's ever done"
◎ 2011: Resigned as CEO of Apple, but remained with the company as chairman of the board until his death

Personal Life Themes/Beliefs

◎ A natural food lover
◎ Embraced Buddhism and New Age philosophy but unable to achieve serenity in his own being
◎ Experimented with psychedelics, later calling his LSD experiences "one of the two or three most important things he had done in his life"
◎ Loved his family but put much of his energy into his work
◎ Advocated the idea that if you build a better product, the consumer will buy it

Selected Quotations

◎ "A lot of companies have chosen to downsize, and maybe that was the right thing for them. We chose a different path. Our belief was that if we kept putting great products in front of customers, they would continue to open their wallets."
◎ "A lot of times, people don't know what they want until you show it to them."
◎ "A lot of people in our industry haven't had very diverse experiences. So they don't have enough dots to connect, and they end up with very linear solutions without a broad perspective on the problem. The broader one's understanding of the human experience, the better design we will have."
◎ "Again, you can't connect the dots looking forward; you can only connect them looking backwards. So you have to trust that the dots will somehow connect in your future. You have to trust in something—your gut, destiny, life, karma, whatever. This approach has never let me down, and it has made all the difference in my life."
◎ "An iPod, a phone, an Internet mobile communicator . . . these are NOT three separate devices! And we are calling it iPhone! Today Apple is going to reinvent the phone. And here it is."
◎ "And it comes from saying no to 1,000 things to make sure we don't get on the wrong track or try to do too much. We're always thinking about

new markets we could enter, but it's only by saying no that you can concentrate on the things that are really important."

◎ "And no, we don't know where it will lead. We just know there's something much bigger than any of us here."

◎ "Apple's market share is bigger than BMW's or Mercedes's or Porsche's in the automotive market. What's wrong with being BMW or Mercedes?"

◎ "But Apple really beats to a different drummer. I used to say that Apple should be the Sony of this business, but in reality, I think Apple should be the Apple of this business."

◎ "As individuals, people are inherently good. I have a somewhat more pessimistic view of people in groups. And I remain extremely concerned when I see what's happening in our country, which is in many ways the luckiest place in the world. We don't seem to be excited about making our country a better place for our kids."

◎ "Be a yardstick of quality. Some people aren't used to an environment where excellence is expected."

◎ "Being the richest man in the cemetery doesn't matter to me. Going to bed at night saying we've done something wonderful, that's what matters to me."

◎ "If you haven't found it yet, keep looking. Don't settle. As with all matters of the heart, you'll know when you find it. And, like any great relationship, it just gets better and better as the years roll on."

◎ "I'm an optimist in the sense that I believe humans are noble and honorable, and some of them are really smart. I have a very optimistic view of individuals."

◎ "I think we're having fun. I think our customers really like our products. And we're always trying to do better."

◎ "Everyone here has the sense that right now is one of those moments when we are influencing the future."

◎ "Computers themselves, and software yet to be developed, will revolutionize the way we learn."

◎ "I didn't see it then, but it turned out that getting fired from Apple was the best thing that could have ever happened to me. The heaviness of being successful was replaced by the lightness of being a beginner again, less sure about everything. It freed me to enter one of the most creative periods of my life."

Awards and Recognition

◎ 1985: Received National Medal of Technology
◎ 1987: Received Samuel S. Beard Award
◎ 1989: Named Entrepreneur of the Decade by *Inc.* magazine
◎ 2007: Named Most Powerful Person in Business by *Fortune* magazine

- 2007: Inducted into the California Hall of Fame
- 2009: Selected as the most admired entrepreneur among teenagers in a survey by Junior Achievement
- 2009: Named CEO of the decade by *Fortune* magazine
- 2010: Ranked No. 17 on *Forbes*: The World's Most Powerful People List
- 2010: Named Person of the Year by *Financial Times*
- 2012: Awarded the Grammy Trustees Award
- 2012: Named the "greatest entrepreneur of our time" by *Fortune* magazine

Death and Aftermath

- Died at his California home around 3 p.m. on October 5, 2011, due to complications from a relapse of pancreatic cancer at the age of 56
- Buried at Alta Mesa Memorial Park, Palo Alto, CA
- Survived by his biological mother, sister Mona Simpson; daughter Lisa Brennan-Jobs; wife Laurene, and their three children, Erin, Reed, and Eve

Lasting Impact and Contributions

- Best known as the co-founder, chairman, and chief executive officer of Apple, Inc. which recently became the most valuable company on Earth
- Jobs's brilliance, passion, and energy were the source of countless innovations that enrich and improve all of our lives
- Was widely described as a visionary, pioneer, and genius, perhaps one of the foremost in the fields of business innovation and product design; profoundly changed the face of the modern world, revolutionized at least six different industries, and was an "exemplar for all chief executives"

Teachers' Rap Sheet

Dwight D. Eisenhower

Full Name: Dwight David Eisenhower

Life Span: Oct. 14, 1890–March 28, 1969

Early Family Background and Created Family Structure

◎ Born in Denison, TX, the third of seven sons born to David and Ida Stover Eisenhower
◎ 1896: lost his 3-year-old brother to diphtheria
◎ Parents were Mennonites
◎ 1897: Family moved to Abilene, KS, where his boyhood home is preserved
◎ 1916: Married Mamie Geneva Doud, 9 months after meeting her
◎ 1917: First child, Doud Dwight born; died at age 3 of scarlet fever
◎ 1922: Second son, John Sheldon Doud, born; had a career in the military and was Ambassador to Belgium

Education

◎ 1909: Graduated from Abilene High School in Kansas
◎ Worked 2 years to help put his brother through college
◎ Took and passed entrance exams for both Annapolis and West Point
◎ 1911: Received appointment to West Point
◎ Smoked too much, studied too little, and received many demerits in defiance of the curtailment of his football playing
◎ Emerged as junior varsity football coach, showing leadership potential
◎ 1915: Graduated in upper half of class
◎ 1926: Graduated from Army's elite graduate school at Ft. Leavenworth, KS, first in his class of 245
◎ 1928: Graduated from Army War College
◎ 1929: Graduated from Army Industrial College

Personality Characteristics and Areas of Aptitude, Talent, and Interest

◎ Energetic, fun-loving, and handsome as a young cadet
◎ Developed a thoughtful, serious, conscientious, subdued approach to power
◎ Saw the value of working behind the scenes and gave credit to others for their involvement and contributions
◎ In his military career, became a great strategist and effective diplomat
◎ Excelled academically when he put his mind to it
◎ Was a star football player at West Point but sidelined by a knee injury

◎ Fascinated with the history of the American West

◎ Enjoyed golf and painting in retirement

Major Career/Professional Events and Accomplishments

◎ 1915: Commissioned second lieutenant and assigned to Ft. Sam Houston, TX

◎ In early career, had multiple postings across the U.S. but prevented from seeing combat duty in World War I despite many requests on his part to be sent overseas

◎ 1922–1924: Served as executive officer to General Fox Connor in the Panama Canal Zone; Connor became his mentor

◎ 1929: Reported to the War Department in Washington, DC, to develop a plan to mobilize manpower and materials to prepare for another war should one occur

◎ 1933: Served as chief military aide to Douglas MacArthur

◎ 1935–1939: Stationed in Philippines under MacArthur with frustrating assignment to build a viable Filipino army

◎ 1940–1941: Stationed in Ft. Lewis, WA, and drew on his expertise of 25 years in the military

◎ Promoted to Brigadier General (one star) a few months before the bombing of Pearl Harbor

◎ 1941: Transferred to War Plans Division in Washington, DC, and promoted to Major General (two stars) the following year

◎ 1942: Arrived in England on a special mission to build cooperation among the Allies in the European Theater as Commanding General; appointed to Lieutenant General (three stars)

◎ 1943: Promoted to General (four stars);. named Commander-in-Chief of Allied Forces North Africa and carried out Operation Torch

◎ 1943: Commanded Allied invasion of Sicily and Italy; planned D-Day invasion of the continent, Operation Overlord

◎ 1943: Appointed Supreme Commander of Allied Expeditionary Forces

◎ 1944: Appointed as a five-star general

◎ 1945: Oversaw unconditional surrender of German High Command and appointed Military Governor of U.S. Occupied Zone

◎ 1945: Selected as Chief of Staff of U.S. Army

◎ 1948–1950: President of Columbia University; stayed involved in decision making on post-war national security policy

◎ 1950: Appointed First Supreme Allied Commander of North Atlantic Treaty Organization (NATO); built the organization around the idea of "concerted, collective unified action"

◎ The grassroots "Draft Eisenhower" presidential effort swelled to a crescendo and he eventually retired from the military to pursue the Republican bid for the presidency

◎ 1952: Elected 34th President of the United States
◎ 1956: Reelected by an even wider margin; peace and prosperity became the watchwords of his presidency
◎ 1957: Congress and the President formed Defense Advanced Research Projects Agency to compete with Russians on space travel
◎ 1957: Ordered federal troops to Little Rock to support the desegregation of Little Rock Central High School
◎ Worked behind the scenes to see Senator Joe McCarthy defeated
◎ 1961: Retired to Gettysburg Farm in Pennsylvania

Personal Life Themes/Beliefs

◎ Joined the Presbyterian church while in office
◎ Was a conservative Republican president; regretted appointing Earl Warren to the Supreme Court (also appointed Brennan)
◎ Believed politics is a profession that is serious, complicated, and ultimately noble
◎ Believed freedom is a value worth preserving at any cost
◎ Believed people who want to maintain a democracy have a responsibility to be informed and active citizens
◎ Optimistic in believing man can create peaceful alternatives to complex problems and disagreements

Selected Quotations

◎ "The qualities of a great man are vision, integrity, courage, understanding, the power of articulation, and profundity of character."
◎ "Humility must always be the portion of any man who receives acclaim earned in the blood of his followers and the sacrifices of his friends."
◎ "Leadership is the art of getting someone else to do something you want done because he wants to do it."
◎ "You do not lead by hitting people over the head. That's assault, not leadership."
◎ "If a problem cannot be solved, enlarge it."
◎ "The older I get the more wisdom I find in the ancient rule of taking first things first, a process that often reduces the most complex human problem to a manageable proportion."
◎ "In preparing for battle I have always found that plans are useless, but planning is indispensable."
◎ "I hate war as only a soldier who has lived it, only as one who has seen its brutality, its futility, its stupidity."
◎ "Every gun that is made, every warship launched, every rocket fired, signifies in the final sense a theft from those who hunger and are not fed, those who are cold and are not clothed."

◎ "Disarmament, with mutual honor and confidence, is a continuing imperative."

◎ "In the councils of government we must guard against the acquisition of unwarranted influence, whether sought or unsought, by the military-industrial complex. The potential for the disastrous rise of misplaced power exists and will persist."

◎ "In the final choice, a soldier's pack is not so heavy as a prisoner's chains."

◎ "A people that values its privileges above its principles soon loses both."

◎ "History does not entrust the care of freedom to the weak or the timid."

◎ "Don't join the book burners. Do not think you are going to conceal thoughts by concealing evidence that they ever existed."

◎ "How has retirement affected my golf game? A lot more people beat me now."

Awards and Recognition

◎ 1918: Received the Army Distinguished Service Medal; later received the Navy Distinguished Service Medal

◎ Following conclusion of the war, he was an international celebrity honored by parades, speeches, and the like

◎ Received numerous national and international military and civic awards, including World War II Service Medal, National Defense Victory Medal, Austrian Order of Merit, French Order of Liberation, Mexican Orders of Military and Civic Merit, Philippines Distinguished Service Star, and USSR Order of Victory Star

◎ 1966: Received Civitan's International World Citizenship Award

◎ 1977: Had an aircraft carrier named after him

◎ Has had many streets and avenues around the world named after him

◎ 1968: Gallop Poll listed him as most admired man in America

◎ 1999: Listed as one of most widely admired people of 20th century

◎ 2009: Named to the World Golf Hall of Fame in the lifetime achievement category

Death and Aftermath

◎ His last year was spent at Walter Reed Army Hospital with a failing heart

◎ Buried in Abilene, KS, in a small chapel on the grounds of the Eisenhower Presidential Library and Museum

◎ A national monument has been commissioned for a site in Washington, DC, in his honor, but plans have stalled

Lasting Impact and Contributions

- For White, middle-class Americans, the era of the Eisenhower presidency was halcyon; he oversaw a period of great economic prosperity, low inflation, low unemployment, and economic growth
- Was much revered by conservatives; liberals were more critical of the lack of progress made on social issues
- Had a significant role in achieving the victory of the Allied forces in World War II but his military strategy capability was criticized by many of his contemporaries
- Set the stage for the reconstruction of Europe and Asia that followed the war; ended the war in Korea
- Supported and signed the 1957 and 1960 Civil Rights Acts, precursors to the major act passed and signed during the Johnson administration
- 1953: Created the Health, Education, and Welfare Department (HEW); expanded Social Security and increased the minimum wage
- During his presidency, the Interstate Highway System was created as well as the National Aeronautics and Space Administration (NASA)
- Oversaw a welcome period of peace in the United States and resisted getting dragged into new military conflicts

Teachers' Rap Sheet

Thurgood Marshall

Full Name: Thurgood Marshall

Life Span: July 2, 1908–January 24, 1993

Early Family Background and Created Family Structure

◎ Born in Baltimore, MD, to William Marshall and Norma Arica
◎ Father was a railroad porter for the Baltimore and Ohio Railroad; mother was an elementary teacher
◎ Home life was modest but both grandfathers owned grocery stores
◎ Great-grandson of a slave
◎ Paternal grandfather joined Union Army as a free man
◎ Born Thoroughgood Marshall, but changed first name in second grade to Thurgood
◎ Had one older brother, William Aubrey Marshall, who become an eminent chest surgeon
◎ Parents instilled in him from youth an appreciation for the United States Constitution and the rule of law
◎ 1929: Married Vivian "Buster" Burey (died from cancer in February 1955)
◎ 1955: Married Cecilia Suyat; had two sons, Thurgood, Jr. and John William
◎ Survived by his wife, Cecilia, two sons, and grandchildren

Education

◎ Attended Baltimore's Colored High and Training School
◎ 1930: Received B.A. from Lincoln University in Pennsylvania (graduated cum laude)
◎ Member of the first Black fraternity, Alpha Phi Alpha
◎ 1933: Received L.L.B. from Howard University School of Law (graduated first in his class, magna cum laude)

Personality Characteristics and Areas of Aptitude, Talent, and Interest

◎ As a child, had a passion for debating law cases with father and brother
◎ Star member of high school debate team
◎ While in high school, he was known for being a mischievous troublemaker
◎ Greatest high school accomplishment was memorizing the entire United States Constitution, which was punishment for misbehaving in class

- Known for being a cutup at Lincoln University, he was thrown out of college twice for fraternity pranks
- Enjoyed poetry and music
- As he aged, was seen as a curmudgeon; reserved and aloof

Major Career/Professional Events and Accomplishments

- 1933: Admitted to the Maryland Bar
- 1934–1938: Set up private practice in Baltimore, MD
- 1935: Won first major civil rights case, *Murray v. Pearson*, desegregating the University of Maryland Law School (the law school Marshall could not attend on the grounds of race)
- 1936: Began working with the National Association for the Advancement of Colored People (NAACP) in Baltimore
- 1939–1941: Served as director of the NAACP's Legal Defense and Education Fund
- 1940s: Was asked by the United Nations and the United Kingdom to help draft the constitutions of the emerging African nations of Ghana and what is now Tanzania
- 1940: Won *Chambers v. Florida*, the first of 29 Supreme Court victories
- 1951: Visited South Korea and Japan to investigate charges of racism in the U.S. Armed Forces; reported that the general practice was one of "rigid segregation"
- 1954: Won *Brown v. Board of Education*, landmark case that demolishes legal basis for segregation of schools in America
- 1960s: Helped draft Bill of Rights for Kenya
- 1961: Appointed by President John F. Kennedy to the United States Court of Appeals for the Second Circuit to a newly created seat
- 1965: Appointed by President Lyndon B. Johnson to be the United States Solicitor General, making him the first African American to hold the office; won 14 out of the 19 cases that he argued for the government
- 1967–1991: Became the first African American appointed as an Associate Justice of the United States Supreme Court
- 1991: Retired from the Supreme Court

Personal Life Themes/Beliefs

- Core values included qualities of thoroughness, excellence, justice, and equality
- Developed a profound sensitivity to injustice by way of the crucible of racial discrimination
- Opposed the death penalty
- Dignified and solemn in manner, but endowed with a sense of humor
- Was an Episcopalian

◎ Portrayed homely virtues and a deep reverence for God

Selected Quotations

◎ "Our whole constitutional heritage rebels at the thought of giving government the power to control men's minds."
◎ "In recognizing the humanity of our fellow beings, we pay ourselves the highest tribute."
◎ "Equal means getting the same thing, at the same time, and in the same place."
◎ "None of us got where we are solely by pulling ourselves up by our bootstraps. We got here because somebody—a parent, a teacher, an Ivy League crony or a few nuns—bent down and helped us pick up our boots."
◎ "The measure of a country's greatness is its ability to retain compassion in times of crisis."
◎ "Ending racial discrimination in jury selection can be accomplished only by eliminating peremptory challenges entirely."
◎ "Mere access to the courthouse doors does not by itself assure a proper functioning of the adversary process."
◎ "What is the quality of your intent?"
◎ "A child born to a Black mother in a state like Mississippi . . . has exactly the same rights as a white baby born to the wealthiest person in the United States. It's not true, but I challenge anyone to say it is not a goal worth working for."
◎ "History teaches that grave threats to liberty often come in times of urgency, when constitutional rights seem too extravagant to endure."

Awards and Recognition

◎ 1946: Received NAACP's Spingarn Medal
◎ 1948: Received The Negro Newspaper Publisher Association's Russwurm Medal
◎ 1950: Received the Living Makers of Negro History Award from the Iota Phi Lambda Sorority
◎ 1969: Received the Horatio Alger Award
◎ 1976: Texas Southern University's law school renamed after him
◎ 1980: University of Maryland School of Law opened a new library named the Thurgood Marshall Law Library
◎ 1992: Received the Liberty Medal
◎ 1993: Received the Presidential Medal of Freedom
◎ 2000: Historic Twelfth Street YMCA Building located in the Shaw neighborhood of Washington, DC, renamed the Thurgood Marshall Center

◎ 2005: International airport serving Baltimore and Maryland areas renamed the Baltimore-Washington International Thurgood Marshall Airport

◎ Name inscribed on the honor roll of the Schomburg History Collection of New York for the advancement of race relations

◎ Held more than 20 honorary degrees from educational institutions in America and abroad

Death and Aftermath

◎ Died of heart failure at the National Naval Medical Center in Bethesda, MD, at the age of 84; buried in Arlington National Cemetery

◎ An obituary read: "We make movies about Malcolm X, we get a holiday to honor Dr. Martin Luther King, but every day we live with the legacy of Justice Thurgood Marshall."

◎ Left all of his personal papers and notes to the Library of Congress

Lasting Impact and Contributions

◎ Best remembered for his high success rate in arguing before the Supreme Court and for the victory in *Brown v. Board of Education* that revolutionized American education and ultimately society

◎ Argued more cases before the United States Supreme Court than anyone else in history

◎ Known for jurisprudence in the fields of civil rights and criminal procedure

◎ One of the greatest and most important figures of the American Civil Rights Movement

Teachers' Rap Sheet

Maya Lin

Full Name: Maya Ying Lin

Life Span: October 5, 1959 to Present

Early Family Background and Created Family Structure

- Born in Athens, OH, to Henry Huan Lin and Julia Chang Lin
- Parents immigrated to the United States from China just before the Communist Revolution of 1949; mother smuggled out on a junk boat to study at Smith College
- Parents were faculty members at Ohio University, College of Fine Arts; father was a ceramicist and Dean of the School of Art and mother is a poet and retired professor of Asian and English literature
- Youngest of two children; older brother is an English professor and poet
- Niece of Lin Huivin, first female architect in China, who helped design Tiananmen Square
- During her childhood, entertained herself by reading and building miniature towns
- Married to Daniel Wolf, New York photography dealer
- Has two daughters, India and Rachel

Education

- Graduated co-valedictorian of her high school in Athens, OH
- 1981: Received B.A. from Yale University
- 1986: Received master's degree from Yale University

Personality Characteristics and Areas of Aptitude, Talent, and Interest

- Has a passion for animals, geology, and the Earth
- Has a talent for mathematics and art
- Loved school—reading and studying
- Took college-level courses during high school
- Spent free time casting bronzes and silversmithing in school foundry
- Is an articulate and compelling speaker
- Loved to hike and bird watch as a child
- Has fundamentally antisocial tendencies; reclusive as a child

Major Career/Professional Events and Accomplishments

- 1981: Won a nationwide competition sponsored by the Vietnam Veterans Memorial Fund to create a design for a monument honoring those who had served and died in that war
- 1982: Completed Vietnam Veterans Memorial in Washington, DC
- 1985: Created a subtle foray into environmental art, placing aluminum rods among reeds at bend of a stream for intercession in the natural environment in West Rock Park, New Haven, CT, named Aligning Reeds
- 1988–1989: Designed a monument for the Civil Rights Movement on behalf of the Southern Poverty Law Center
- 1989–1989: Created Open-Air Peace Chapel for Juniata College, which is two related stone circles on a rural hilltop site
- 1989–1991: Worked on Topo for the Charlotte Sports Coliseum, featuring earthworks and topiaries
- 1989–1995: Created Eclipsed Time for the Pennsylvania Station, featuring a ceiling clock whose face gradually darkens between noon and midnight, and then slowly brightens again in the morning hours
- 1992–1993: Appointed visual artist-in-residence at the Peter Eisenman's Wexner Center at Ohio State University; created Groundswell, wave forms sculpted from recycled safety glass
- 1993: Completed Women's Table for Yale University, featuring a granite water table honoring the women of Yale with a spiral, engraved timeline that records the number of women in Yale programs from the founding of the school in early 18th century to 1993
- 1993–1995: Worked on the Wave Field for the FXB Aerospace Engineering Building at the University of Michigan, which was a tract of land sculpted into forms reminiscent of water waves
- 1996–1998: Created Reading a Garden for the Cleveland Public Library in collaboration with brother, Tan Lin, which is an interactive outdoor garden space melding sculptural environment with abstract poetry
- 1999: Commissioned to remodel a barn to accommodate the 5,000-volume Langston Hughes Library on civil rights and children's advocacy for The Children's Defense Fund
- 2000–2001: Designed The Character of a Hill, Under Glass for the American Express Client Services Center, which contains a garden inside a three-story glass box in the front lobby featuring an exterior wall turned into a waterfall which freezes in winter
- 2004: Completed Input at Ohio University, a park that resembles an old-fashioned computer punch card when seen from the air
- 2005: Created Flutter, an earthwork of soil and grass that rises and falls in waves as if to give the building a surface to float upon, at the federal courthouse in Miami, FL

◎ 2007: Installed Above and Below, an outdoor sculpture at the Indianapolis Museum of Art

◎ 2009: Unveiled Silver River at the Aria in Las Vegas; 87-foot-long representation, cast in reclaimed silver, of the entire length of the Colorado River hangs luminously over the registration desk, making a statement about water conservation

◎ 2009: Completed the design for the Museum of Chinese in America's new space in Manhattan's Chinatown

◎ 2012: Working on a multimedia, multisite memorial that aims to build awareness about species loss and highlight what scientists and environmental groups throughout the world are doing to protect species and habitats

Personal Life Themes/Beliefs

◎ Has a strong interest in conservation; goal in her landscape art is to cooperate with nature rather than try to overpower it and bend it to her will

◎ Goal has been to design with honesty, individual loss, legacy, and tribute in mind

◎ Sees her work as "an idea without a shape"

◎ Describes architecture as being "surrounded by problem solving" and "like a puzzle"

Selected Quotations

◎ "Sometimes I think creativity is magic; it's not a matter of finding an idea, but allowing the idea to find you."

◎ "To fly we have to have resistance."

◎ "For the most part things never get built the way they were drawn."

◎ "It terrified me to have an idea that was solely mine, to be no longer a part of my mind, but totally public."

◎ "The definition of a modern approach to war is the acknowledgement of individual lives lost."

◎ "The role of art in society differs for every artist."

◎ "Art is very tricky because it's what you do for yourself. It's much harder for me to make those works than the monuments or the architecture. "

◎ "Sometimes you have to stop thinking. Sometimes you shut down completely. I think that's true in any creative field."

◎ "To me, the American Dream is being able to follow your own personal calling. To be able to do what you want to do is incredible freedom."

◎ "You have to let the viewers come away with their own conclusions. If you dictate what they should think, you've lost it."

◎ "All my work is much more peaceful than I am."

◎ "Every memorial in its time has a different goal."

◎ "I try to give people a different way of looking at their surroundings. That's art to me."

◎ "I like to think of my work as creating a private conversation with each person; no matter how public each work is and no matter how many people are present."

Awards and Recognition

◎ 1995: Subject of the Academy Award-winning documentary, *Maya Lin: A Strong Clear Vision*, which won Oscar for best documentary

◎ 2002: Elected Alumni Fellow of the Yale Corporation

◎ 2003: Served on the selection jury of the World Trade Center Site Memorial Competition

◎ 2005: Became a member of the American Academy of Arts and Letters

◎ 2005: Inducted into the National Women's Hall of Fame

◎ 2005: Became a member of the American Academy of Arts and Sciences

◎ 2009: Awarded the National Medal of Arts

◎ Awarded Henry Bacon Memorial Award

◎ Served on the Board of Energy Foundation

◎ Awarded the Presidential Design Award

◎ Received American Institute of Architects Honor Award

◎ Served on the National Advisory Board to the Presidio Council in San Francisco

◎ Received the Thomas Jefferson Foundation Medal in Architecture

◎ 2009: Awarded the National Medal of Arts by President Obama

◎ Board member on the Natural Resources Defense Council

◎ Architecture and artworks have consistently elicited praise and received awards

◎ Awarded honorary doctorate degrees from Yale University, Harvard University, Williams College, and Smith College

◎ Among youngest at Yale University to receive an honorary Doctorate of Fine Arts

Lasting Impact and Contributions

◎ Best known for her design of the Vietnam Veterans Memorial in Washington, DC

◎ Has designed several of the most significant and best-known works of public art of the late 20th century

◎ Her gift is creating work that rethinks human relationships to Earth and time

◎ Integrates a scientific and/or historic component into a living form, a reminder to treasure Earth and stone, time and space

- ◎ Work originates from a simple desire to make people aware of their surroundings, not just the physical but the psychological world where we live
- ◎ Her vision and focus is always on how the space needs to be in the future and what it means to the people
- ◎ Incorporates recycled, living, and other natural materials in her work
- ◎ Bringing awareness of the enormous loss of species that is presently occurring, with equal attention on the threatened habitats and ecosystems that are vital to other species' survival
- ◎ Brought awareness to the world of the diminished sounds of songbirds that were common in her childhood, even the visibility of the stars at night

Teachers' Rap Sheet
Nikola Telsa

Full Name: Nikola Tesla

Life Span: July 10, 1856–January 7, 1943

Early Family Background and Created Family Structure

- Born in the mountainous village of Smiljan, Lika (now part of Gospic, present-day Croatia)
- A subject of the Austrian Empire by birth and later became an American citizen
- Parents were both Serbian by origin
- Father, Milutin Tesla, was a priest in the Serbian Orthodox Church and a gifted writer and poet
- Mother, Djuka Mandic Tesla created appliances to help with home and farm responsibilities; never learned to read, but memorized many Serbian epic poems
- Fourth of five children; had one older brother and three sisters
- As a young boy, he immersed himself in his father's library
- Had an interest in how things worked; made fish hooks, a waterwheel, a pop gun, and swords, among other things, as a child
- Encouraged by father to enter the priesthood
- At age 17, contracted cholera
- Attributed his inventive instincts to his mother
- 1891: Became a naturalized citizen of the United States of America
- Lifelong bachelor; devoted his full energies to science

Education

- Attended Higher Real Gymnasium (secondary) in Karlovac where he finished a 4-year term in 3 years
- 1879: Received a Baccalaureate of Physics, Baccalaureate of Mathematics, Baccalaureate of Mechanical Engineering, and Baccalaureate of Electrical Engineering from Austrian Polytechnic Institute (Graz)
- Received a Ph.D. in physics from University of Prague

Personality Characteristics and Areas of Aptitude, Talent, and Interest

- Could read both the Cyrillic and Latin alphabet before first grade
- Had a keen memory and ability to visualize and construct complicated objects in his mind's eye
- Learned, by heart, 144 poems, ballads, and pieces from the liturgy books

◎ Was passionate about mathematics and sciences
◎ Was able to perform integral calculus in his mind, prompting his teachers to think he was cheating
◎ Was a strikingly handsome, tall, slender man who exhibited unusual powers of perception and forecasting
◎ Was a captivating public lecturer
◎ Was fluent in seven languages (English, Serbian, Croatian, Hungarian, French, German, Italian)
◎ Had a complete nervous breakdown after studies at Austrian Polytechnic Institute

Major Career/Professional Events and Accomplishments

◎ 1881: Became the chief electrician to the National Telephone Company in Budapest, where he made his first invention, a telephone repeater, and conceived the idea of a rotating magnetic field
◎ 1882: Moved to Paris to work as an engineer for the Continental Edison Company designing improvements to electric equipment; in addition, discovered the rotating magnetic field, a fundamental principle for devices using alternating current, and constructed a working brushless polyphase AC induction motor
◎ 1884: Accepted a job with the Edison Company in New York City to make improvements in Edison's dynamos and redesign the inferior construction for $50,000
◎ 1885: After completing job, Edison reneged on promise to pay the monies for improvements and Tesla quit
◎ 1886: Formed his own company, Tesla Electric Light & Manufacturing; initial financial investors disagreed with Tesla on his plan for an alternating current motor and eventually relieved Tesla of his duties at the company
◎ 1887: Filed for seven U.S. patents in the field of polyphase AC motors and power transmission; comprised a complete system of generators, transformers, transmission lines, motors, and lighting, the most valuable patents since the telephone
◎ 1888: Sold George Westinghouse polyphase patents and, in addition to monies, received stock in Westinghouse Corporation; Tesla set 60 cycles per second (now Hertz) as the North American standard for AC power transmission and distribution
◎ 1891: Built own experimental laboratory in New York City, where he developed the principles of the Tesla Coil, an electrical resonant transformer circuit used to produce high voltage, low current, high frequency alternating current electricity

- 1892–1894: Served as the vice president of the Institute of Electrical and Electronics Engineers
- 1892: Was granted 40 patents, locking in his rotating magnetic field principles and polyphase power distribution into a comprehensive system for the generation, transmission, distribution, and utilization of AC power
- 1892: Discovered X-ray radiation while experimenting with HV and evacuated tube
- 1896: *The Electrical Review* published X-rays of a man, made by Tesla, with X-ray tubes of his own design
- 1893: Made the first public demonstration of radio communication in St. Louis, MO (wireless transmitter/receiver); 2 years before Marconi's first demonstration
- 1893: Tesla and Westinghouse astonished the world by demonstrating the wonders of alternating current electricity at the World Columbia Exposition in Chicago; President Cleveland pushed a button and a hundred thousand incandescent lamps illuminated the buildings
- 1895–1896: Designed the first hydroelectric power plant, the final victory of alternating current
- 1897: Patented the basic system of radio; his published schematic diagrams describing all the basic elements of the radio transmitter
- 1898: Developed the "art of telautomatics," a form of robotics, as well as the technology of remote control, which demonstrated a wireless radio-controlled boat to the U.S. military
- 1898: Developed electric igniter for gasoline engines; basically the same approach that's used in today's internal combustion engines
- 1899: Built a laboratory station in Colorado Springs, CO, to experiment with high voltage, high frequency electricity, and other phenomena; researched ways to transmit power and energy wirelessly over long distances
- 1906–1911: Demonstrated his patents for a bladeless steam turbine based on a spiral flow principle and his pump design to operate at extremely high temperature
- 1912: Refused the Nobel Prize for Physics, stating he would not share this honor with Edison, and Marconi had already received what should have been Tesla's prize.
- 1928: Received his last patent, "Apparatus for Aerial Transportation," similar to a helicopter
- 1956: The "Tesla," a new unit of magnetic flux density in the metric system, is named in his honor—the new unit is equivalent to 10,000 Gauss

Personal Life Themes/Beliefs

- Required little sleep—usually 2 hours a night
- Was fastidious about cleanliness and hygiene
- Inherited from his father a deep hatred of war; throughout his life, he sought a technological way to end warfare
- Showed up for work every day in formal dress
- Was an appreciator of fine music
- Was a brilliant and eccentric man who suffered from obsessive-compulsive disorder

Selected Quotations

- "The gift of mental power comes from God, Divine being, and if we concentrate our minds on that truth, we become in tune with this great power."
- "We build but to tear down. Most of our work and resource is squandered. Our onward march is marked by devastation. Everywhere there is an appalling loss of time, effort and life. A cheerless view, but true."
- "If your hate could be turned into electricity, it would light up the whole world."
- "I do not think there is any thrill that can go through the human heart like that felt by the inventor as he sees some creation of the brain unfolding to success . . . such emotions make a man forget food, sleep, friends, love, everything."
- "Let the future tell the truth, and evaluate each one according to his work and accomplishments. The present is theirs; the future, for which I have really worked, is mine."
- "Our virtues and our failings are inseparable, like force and matter. When they separate, man is no more."
- "The scientists of today think deeply instead of clearly. One must be sane to think clearly, but one can think deeply and be quite insane."
- "The practical success of an idea, irrespective of its inherent merit, is dependent on the attitude of the contemporaries. If timely, it is quickly adopted; if not, it is apt to fare like a sprout lured out of the ground by warm sunshine, only to be injured and retarded in its growth by the succeeding frost."
- "The spread of civilization may be likened to a fire; first, a feeble spark, next a flickering flame, then a mighty blaze, ever increasing in speed and power."
- "Today's scientists have substituted mathematics for experiments, and they wander off through equation after equation, and eventually build a structure which has no relation to reality."
- "My method is different. I do not rush into actual work. When I get a new idea, I start at once building it up in my imagination, and make

improvements and operate the device in my mind. When I have gone so far as to embody everything in my invention, every possible improvement I can think of, and when I see no fault anywhere, I put into concrete form the final product of my brain."

◎ "Like a flash of lightning and in an instant the truth was revealed, I drew with a stick on the sand the diagrams of my motor. A thousand secrets of nature which I might have stumbled upon accidentally, I would have given for that one which I had wrestled from her against all odds and at the peril of my existence."

◎ "If Edison had a needle to find in a haystack, he would proceed at once with the diligence of the bee to examine straw after straw until he found the object of his search. I was a sorry witness of such doings, knowing that a little theory and calculation would have saved him ninety percent of his labor."

Awards and Recognition

◎ 1892: Awarded the Order of St. Sava
◎ 1894: Awarded the Elliott Cresson Medal
◎ 1894: Awarded honorary doctoral degrees from Yale and Columbia
◎ 1895: Awarded the Order of Danilo
◎ 1917: Awarded the Edison Medal, most coveted electrical prize in the United States
◎ 1931: Was on the cover of *TIME Magazine*
◎ 1934: Awarded the John Scott Medal
◎ 1952: The Nikola Tesla Museum, Belgrade, Serbia was founded
◎ 1952: 2244 Tesla, a minor planet, was named for Nikola Tesla
◎ 1976: The Nikola Tesla Monument given to U.S. by Yugoslavia celebrating the first hydroelectric plant at Niagara Falls
◎ 1975: Inducted into the Inventor's Hall of Fame
◎ The Nikola Tesla award is one of the most distinguished honors presented by the Institute of Electrical Engineers (annually given since 1976)
◎ 1983: Honored with a commemorative stamp
◎ 1984: The rock band Tesla derived its name and certain album and song titles from events relating to him
◎ 1997: Named one of the 100 most famous people of the last 1,000 years—citing him as one of the most farsighted inventors of the electrical age in *LIFE Magazine's* special issue
◎ 2003: Tesla Motors, an electric car company, takes its name from him
◎ 2005: Listed among the top 100 nominees in the TV show The Greatest American
◎ 2006: Serbia (Belgrade) airport was renamed Belgrade Nikola Tesla Airport

◎ 2006: Nikola Tesla monument erected on Canadian side of Niagara Falls

◎ 2009: Google honored his birthday by displaying a doodle in the Google search home page that showed the G as a Tesla coil

◎ Awarded the highest order of the White Lion by Czechoslovakia; considered a luminary in the field of science and one of the symbols of personified pride for Eastern Europe

Death and Aftermath

◎ Died from heart thrombus on January 7, 1943, in the Hotel New Yorker, where he had lived his last 10 years of life

◎ A state funeral, conducted in the name of the Serbian Orthodox Church in New York parish, was attended by 2,000 people

◎ Tesla's casket was draped with U.S. and Yugoslav flags; his pallbearers were Nobel Prize winners

◎ Cremated with remains held at Campbell Cemetery until 1957, then his ashes were interned in a golden sphere, Tesla's favorite shape, where they are on permanent display at the Tesla Museum in Belgrade, Serbia along with his death mask

◎ FBI ordered Office of Alien Property to seize Tesla's papers and possessions, as they were declared to be top secret by J. Edgar Hoover; eventually, they were released to his nephew, and are currently housed in the Nikola Tesla Museum in Belgrade, Serbia

Lasting Impact and Contributions

◎ Inventor of the rotating magnetic field and of the complete system of production and distribution of electrical energy (motors, generators) based on the use of alternate currents

◎ First crossover scientist (both scientist and engineer) known and respected in both circles

◎ Transformed America from a nation of isolated communities to a country connected by power grids where information was available upon demand

◎ Gave us technology that united the United States and eventually the world

◎ His legacy can be seen in everything from microwave ovens to MX missiles

◎ Greatest achievement is his polyphase alternating current system, which is today lighting the entire globe

◎ Among his discoveries are the fluorescent light, laser beam, wireless communications, wireless transmission of electrical energy, remote control, and robotics

◎ Registered more than 700 patents worldwide

Appendix B
Annotated Bibliography

Biographic Compendia

Adams, S., Ashe, C., Chrisp, P., Johnson, E., Langley, A., & Weeks, M. (1999). *1000 makers of the millennium*. New York, NY: DK Publishing.

Organized into 10 centuries, the book identifies and provides brief biographies of 1,000 influential people. Many color photographs and illustrations are included. There is a strong contingent of celebrities and sports figures chosen for the late 1900s, which may be a commentary on the times in which we live.

Ashby, R., & Ohrn, D. G. (Eds.). (1995). *Herstory: Women who changed the world*. New York, NY: Viking Press.

This reference book begins with an introductory essay by Gloria Steinem that documents several examples of prejudice against women up through the last half of the 20th century. The book is subdivided into three sections, grouped by time periods: prehistory to 1750; 1750 to 1850; and 1890 to around 1990. The first section contains 21 brief biographies, including Queen Hatshepsut, Sappho, Joan of Arc, Queen Isabella I, and Queen Elizabeth I. Section II contains more than 40 brief biographies including Sacajawea, Sojourner Truth, the Brontë sisters, Clara Barton, Jane Addams, and Beatrix Potter. The third section contains more than 50 brief biographies of women from a wide range of fields. All three sections have introductory essays and are drawn from an international template.

Meadows, J. (1997). *The world's great minds*. London, England: Chancellor Press.

Biographies of 12 great thinkers are presented with supporting information about the times and cultures in which their contributions were embedded. The individuals include Aristotle, Galileo Galilei, William Harvey, Sir Isaac Newton, Antoine Lavoisier, Alexander von Humboldt, Michael Faraday, Charles Darwin, Louis Pasteur, Marie Curie, Sigmund Freud, and Albert Einstein. This text contains many color and black and white photographs and illustrations.

The Editors of Salem Press. (2009). *American heroes* (Vol. 3). Pasadena, CA: The Salem Press.

Sixty-four brief biographies with reference citations are presented alphabetically for American notables whose last names range from Nicklaus to Zacharias. Included are such luminaries as Chester Nimitz, Sandra Day O'Connor, Walter Reed, Jackie Robinson, Eleanor Roosevelt, Sacajawea, and Tecumseh. There are two other volumes of this book that contain brief biographies of leaders included in this curriculum unit. Volume 1 covers heroes whose names range from Aaron to Geronimo. Included in this volume are Jane Addams, Robert Ballard, Clara Barton, Rachel Carson, Cesar Chavez, Walt Disney, Amelia Earhart, Dwight D. Eisenhower, and Bill Gates. Volume 2 ranges from Gibson to Navratilova and includes Steve Jobs.

Time/CBS News. (1999). *People of the century: One hundred men and women who shaped the last one hundred years.* New York, NY: Simon and Schuster.

Biographical information in the context of brief essays is presented on 100 personalities or representatives of ideas that media sources suggested define the 20th century. The people selected range from Sigmund Freud, Emmeline Pankhurst, Theodore Roosevelt, and Henry Ford at the beginning of the 1900s, to Oprah Winfrey, Bill Gates, Bart Simpson, and the "Unknown Tiananmen Square Rebel" at the end of the century. Interesting photographs in both color and black and white are interspersed with the text.

Autobiographies and Biographies on Leaders in the Unit

Cheney, M. (2001). *Tesla: Man out of time.* New York, NY: Touchstone.

This is a very readable biography of Tesla that was first published in the early 1980s: interesting, compact, and well written. Until the recent contribution by Seifer (see below) that was able to incorporate information from previously inaccessible sources, this was the recognized biography of the man; it offers sufficient material to examine Tesla's life and his engineering innovations.

Isaacson, W. (2011). *Steve Jobs.* New York, NY: Simon & Schuster.

This authorized biography was issued shortly after Jobs passed away and made the best-seller lists for nonfiction. Isaacson had extensive access to and discussions with Jobs and interviewed many who knew him personally. The book has been criticized for lacking distance in its perspective, but it is an even-handed treatment of a complex, dynamic, and visionary individual.

Lin, M. (2000). *Boundaries*. New York, NY: Simon & Schuster. (A paperback of this book was printed in 2006.)

This beautiful, coffee-table book is an "abstract" self-portrait of the artist that contains lecture notes, essays, and photographs of 18 of her works.

Seifer, M. J. (2001). *Wizard: The life and times of Nikola Tesla: Biography of a genius*. Secaucus, NJ: Citadel Press.

This is the current definitive biography on Tesla. Long, detailed, well researched and well written, it is filled with interesting details of Tesla's life.

Smith, J. E. (2012). *Eisenhower in war and peace*. New York, NY: Random House.

This work offers a contemporary look back at the life and legacy of our former President.

Williams, J. (2000). *Thurgood Marshall: American revolutionary*. New York, NY: Three Rivers Press.

This is an excellent biography, although several of Marshall's personal connections refused to provide interview data for fear of Marshall's image being tarnished; the book praises Marshall for his enormous contribution to the Civil Rights Movement and is even-handed in its treatment of Marshall's foibles.

Although biographies of Oprah Winfrey are available, the authors of this unit have not reviewed them and are not in a position to make a recommendation at this time.

Research Literature on Leadership

Baldoni J. (2012). *Lead with purpose: Giving your organization a reason to believe in itself*. NY, NY: Amacom.

Based on personal experience, interviews with CEOs and other authorities on leadership, and surveys of 1,100 members of the American Management Association, the author uses the lens of "purpose" as a frame for his ideas about effective leadership. Chapters focus on inspiring purposeful people, turning purpose into results, making it safe to fail, and developing the next generation of leaders. The results from the survey are included in an appendix. The response that got the highest rating when asked how to instill purpose in the workplace was that leaders need to do what they promise. This book may be on the curve of tapping into the disillusionment spawned by the breakdown in values that led to the current recession.

Bethel, S. M. (2009). *A new breed of leader: 8 leadership qualities that matter most in the real world: What works, what doesn't, and why.* New York, NY: Penguin.

The author interviewed 13 leaders from a cross-section of fields and identified eight leadership qualities that matter most in the real world. These are competence, accountability, openness, language, values, perspective, power, and humility. She says that the new breed of leader must be physically strong, mentally quick, politically limber, emotionally stable, and intellectually superior, as well as an unselfish consensus-builder.

Bennis, W., & Goldsmith, J. (2010). *Learning to lead: A workbook on becoming a leader* (4th ed.). New York, NY: Basic Books.

This text identifies four characteristics that are wanted from today's leaders (providing purpose, direction, and meaning; building and sustaining trust; purveying hope and optimism; and delivering results) and offers insights and explication to help managers develop into leaders.

Blank, W. (2001). *The 108 skills of natural born leaders.* New York, NY: Amacom.

Starting with the premise that no one is a born leader, this text identifies 108 skills that can be developed to strengthen leadership capabilities in people. Blank differentiates between people who are managers and people who are leaders. He includes a self-assessment inventory that organizes the 108 skills into nine sets: self-awareness, capacity to develop rapport with people, ability to clarify expectations, ability to map the territory to identify the need to lead, ability to chart a course of leadership action, ability to develop others as leaders, ability to build the base to gain commitment, ability to influence others to willingly follow, and ability to create a motivating environment. The last skill he posits is the ability to continually seek renewal.

Bolman, L. G., & Deal, T. E. (2006). *The wizard and the warrior: Leading with passion and power.* San Francisco, CA: Jossey-Bass.

Based on the authors' work with many contemporary leaders, they suggest that two of the four frames (see next reference) by which leadership is construed need more attention. These two frames are the political, which focuses on the use of power and understanding power relationships, and the symbolic, which focuses on the importance of establishing meaning. They have retitled these two lenses the warrior and the wizard. This text discusses these two frames in more detail. The talents of the warrior are described as heart, mind, skill, and weapons. The wizard's strength is in seeing below the surface and bringing artistry and magic into a potentially sterile environment.

Bolman, L. G., & Deal, T. E. (2008). *Reframing organizations: Artistry, choice, and leadership* (4th ed.). San Francisco, CA: Jossey-Bass.

The authors offer an interesting lens through which to view the leadership construct. They suggest that effective leadership involves making judgments about the combined use of four leadership frames: (1) structural—the role of tasks and organizational hierarchies (architect); (2) human resources—the role of relationship building (catalyst); (3) political—the role of power distribution (advocate); and (4) symbolic—the role of meaning (prophet). They see leadership as situational and change as involving conflict and loss. Their perspective is drawn from the field of business, and they identify the characteristics of high-performing companies.

Clawson, J. G. (2012). *Level three leadership: Getting below the surface* (5th ed.) Upper Saddle River, NJ: Pearson Education.

This text provides a comprehensive discussion of the changes in understanding leadership that have occurred over the last four decades and posits that leadership development has evolved through three stages. Hallmarks of level three leadership are a commitment to purpose and values, decentralization of power, continuous learning and renewal, and rigorous self-reflection and analysis. The author suggests six steps to effective leadership: clarifying your center, clarifying what is possible, clarifying what others can contribute, supporting others so that they can contribute, being relentless, and measuring and celebrating progress. The book contains an excellent appendix on leadership theories that summarizes the major contributions and ideas to the field over the last 35 years.

Cohen, W. A. (2008). *A class with Drucker: The lost lessons of the world's greatest management teacher*. New York, NY: Amacom.

The author, who spent much of his early career in the military, took classes with Drucker, a leading guru in business management in the late 20th century. This book has insightful reflections on the lessons he learned, including the need to build self-confidence step-by-step, that the future cannot be predicted but it can be created, and the distinctions between ethics, honor, integrity, and the law matter. Cohen also shares his own version of the eight universal laws of leadership derived from his study of military leaders who had gone onto success in other fields upon discharge: integrity first, know your stuff, declare your expectations, show uncommon commitment, expect positive results, take care of your people, put duty before self, and get out in front.

Covey, S. R. (2004). *The 7 habits of highly effective people* (Rev. ed.). New York, NY: Simon and Schuster.

This bestseller identifies seven time-honored factors that underscore effective leadership. Covey's synthesis includes (1) being proactive, honoring commitments, and initiating change; (2) developing personal mission statements, setting goals, and identifying desired outcomes; (3) the importance of self-awareness and identity; (4) prioritizing what's important (planning, organizing, time management); (5) win-win relationship-building (character, integrity, trust, cooperation, and honesty); (6) empathic communication (listening and understanding); and (7) creative cooperation (synergy), team-building, and collaboration.

De Pree, M. (1997). *Leading without power: Finding hope in serving community.* San Francisco, CA: Jossey-Bass.

This book is written for organizations that rely on or utilize volunteers and focuses on shared values and commitment, united missions, and moral purpose. De Pree asserts that when people work for love, the leader's role is to help them move toward potential and service to others. He raises the question of what should be measured in these contexts, discusses attributes of vital organizations, and identifies important considerations in regards to the ideas of risk, virtue, and legacy.

Dyer, J. H., Gregersen, H. B., & Christensen, C. M. (2009, December 21). The innovator's DNA. *Harvard Business Review,* 2–8.

This study was based on the habits of 25 innovative entrepreneurs and surveys of 3,000 executives and 500 individuals who had started innovative companies or invented new products. The authors found that innovative business people spend 50% more of their time on a set of discovery-oriented activities than do CEOs with no track record for innovation, and they believe that these skills can be cultivated in others. The five discovery skills they identify are associating, which is a thinking skill, and four "doing" skills (questioning, observing, experimenting, and networking).

Gardner, H. (2011). *Creating minds: An anatomy of creativity seen through the lives of Freud, Einstein, Picasso, Stravinsky, Eliot, Graham, and Gandhi*. New York, NY: Basic Books.

The author uses the study of seven creative individuals drawn from different domains to offer insights on the construct of creativity. He believes that creativity evolves from the interaction of domains, individuals, and fields and that it is novel problem solving within a domain that ultimately becomes accepted. He discusses the criticality of early support and the Faustian bargain that individuals make in order to rise to the top of their fields.

Gladwell, M. (2008). *Outliers: The story of success*. New York, NY: Little, Brown.

The author examines a variety of variables that contribute to or help explain the attainment of success in a variety of fields or enterprises. Chapter 2 of the book discusses the theory of the 10,000-hour rule, a rule that proposes that at least 10,000 hours of study and practice, initiated at a young age, are necessary to achieve a high level of mastery in almost any complex domain or talent arena. One of his examples pertains to Bill Gates's early involvement in programming computers, giving him a foundational skill set that was unusual for his time period but one that culminated in a remarkable career trajectory.

Hamer, D., & Copeland, P. (1998). *Living with our genes: Why they matter more than you think*. New York, NY: Doubleday Books.

Behavioral aptitudes, personality preferences, and individual temperaments are programmed into our genes, but preference does not mean that the behavior will be actualized. True skill mastery requires practice. This understanding of the developmental dimension of leadership underscores the lessons in this curriculum unit.

Hart, L. B., & Waisman, C. S. (2005). *The leadership training activity book: 50 exercises for building effective leaders*. New York, NY: Amacom.

This well-sequenced, well-structured, and clearly formatted workbook, with homage to the management ideas of Kouzes and Posner, contains 50 useful, hands-on activities for leadership training with an adult population. Activities are geared toward key behaviors or concepts in leadership such as storytelling, team-building, ethical decision making, values clarification, embracing change, creative thinking, presenting with pizazz, and acknowledging success.

Kouzes, J. M., & Posner, B. Z. (1999). *The leadership challenge planner: An action guide to achieving your personal best.* San Francisco, CA: Jossey-Bass.

This clear and insightful text identifies five skill sets that define effective leadership. The authors posit that leaders (1) are pioneers and early adopters of innovation who lead the way by challenging the process and taking risks, (2) inspire a shared vision through dialogue, (3) enable others to act through team-building, (4) model the way through careful planning, and (5) encourage and nurture by feedback, praise, celebration, and rewards.

Li, C. (2010). *Open leadership: How social technology can transform the way you lead.* San Francisco, CA: Jossey-Bass.

This book examines the impact social networking sites and the Internet have had on business practices and identifies ways to nurture open leadership in response to the new technological environment that companies find themselves facing.

Linkner, J. (2011). *Disciplined dreaming: A proven system to drive breakthrough creativity.* San Francisco, CA: Jossey-Bass.

Based on his own experience as founder of ePrize and on interviews with CEOs, business people, and artists, the author shares his five-step system for enhancing and promoting creativity within organizations. The main components of his process are ask, prepare, discover, ignite, and launch. His ideas are well grounded in research and practice, and they are presented in a down-to-earth and workable format. The two activities in Lesson 7 in this curriculum unit were created from suggestions in this book.

Mai, R., & Akerson, A. (2003). *The leader as communicator: Strategies and tactics to build loyalty, focus effort, and spark creativity.* New York, NY: Amacom.

This text makes the argument that the primary skill set in effective leadership is related to communication and that leadership communication is about relationship building. It identifies three communication roles for leaders: building community by making meaning, navigating and setting direction, and championing the renewal process. The chapter entitled "Storyteller" relates how the use of stories, anecdotes, and parables can inform and educate as well as inspire.

In addition to the roles of meaning-maker and storyteller, other roles that are highlighted in the text are trust-builder, direction-setter, transition-pilot, linking agent, critic, provocateur, learning advocate, and innovation-coach.

Nanus, B. (1992). *Visionary leadership.* San Francisco, CA: Jossey-Bass.

This primer on leadership endorses the idea that there are differences between managers and leaders (previously posited by Bennis and Goldsmith) and discusses specific characteristics related to the idea of vision, including that a powerful vision is capable of attracting others, creating meaning, establishing excellence, and forecasting future directions. The author believes that leadership is a mix of judgment (structure, assessment, form, and purpose) and instinct (intuition) and that teaching leadership is important at K–12 levels if the U.S. is to be competitive in the 21st century.

Newman, R. (2012). *Rebounders: How winners pivot from setback to success.* New York, NY: Ballantine.

The author uses abbreviated case studies of 12 high-profile people who have rebounded from major setbacks in their careers to examine the habits of mind and behaviors that contribute to resilience. Eleven of his subjects are contemporary individuals drawn from business, sports, politics, and the arts. He offers an iconoclastic take on some of the traditional algorithms associated with leadership while reenforcing others. For instance, he is cautious about the role of passion, suggesting that drive is more important. He downplays optimism in favor of defensive pessimism. He champions the attributes of persistence, patience, and tolerance of failure when used to achieve new levels of insight and personal growth. The book is delightfully readable, offering engaging biographical stories and provocative ideas.

Payne, V. (2001). *The team-building workshop.* New York, NY: Amacom.

This text offers steps, strategies, and exercises in the art of team-building, starting with an understanding of the value of team-building to an organization. It is designed for individuals who are conducting team-building workshops or sessions. Of particular note is the section on resolving team conflict and the inventory of experiential exercises.

Quick, T. L. (1992). *Successful team building.* New York, NY: Amacom.

This how-to manual for team-building offers helpful chapters on the nature and benefits of a team, including characteristics of effective and ineffective teams, building commitment, dealing with conflict, and group problem solving and decision making.

Simonton, D. K. (1994). *Greatness: Who makes history and why.* New York, NY: Guilford Press.

Using historical research as a basis for exploring the concept of greatness, Simonton offers valuable insights that impact the literature on the construct of leadership. Among the ideas he explores are the role of creativity in leadership; human potential and the development of talent (born or learned or situational); the role of models and mentors in leadership; the importance of personality (self-actualizers, extroversion and introversion); early exposure and learning in a field as predictive of later accomplishment; factors of family, education, stimulation, adversity, and marginality; and the role of motivation and drive.

Wallace, D. B., & Gruber, H. E. (1989). *Creative people at work: Twelve cognitive case studies.* New York, NY: Oxford University Press.

This interesting take on creativity discusses ideas that have salience for the research on leadership. The text is organized around four basic themes: (1) an evolving systems approach (organization of knowledge, purpose, and affect) to understanding the construct of creativity in the domain of work, (2) networks of enterprise, (3) the role of novelty and chance, and (4) personal freedom and social responsibility—the twin tensions of creators/leaders (i.e., moral and ethical leadership).

About the Authors

Linda D. Avery, Ph.D., managed the Center for Gifted Education at The College of William and Mary upon receiving her doctorate in educational leadership, policy, and planning from that institution in the late 1990s. Previously she helped establish the first gifted education program at the state level in Michigan and helped administer the long-established state program in Illinois. She has authored language arts curriculum materials based on the Integrated Curriculum Model (ICM) and oversaw the preparation of a collection of social studies curriculum units. She has conducted several state and local gifted program evaluation studies over her career and numerous professional development workshops in curriculum development and implementation. She is currently living in Seville, OH.

Joyce VanTassel-Baska, Ed.D., is the Jody and Layton Smith Professor Emerita at The College of William and Mary, where she developed a graduate program and a research and development center in gifted education. Formerly, she initiated and directed the Center for Talent Development at Northwestern University. She has also served as the state director of gifted programs for Illinois, as a regional director of a gifted service center in the Chicago area, as coordinator of gifted programs for the Toledo, OH, public school system, and as a teacher of gifted high school students in English and Latin. Dr. VanTassel-Baska has published widely, including 27 books and more than 500 refereed journal articles, book chapters, and scholarly reports. Her major research interests are the talent development process and effective curricular interventions with the gifted.

Common Core
State Standards Alignment

Grade Level	Common Core State Standards
Grade 9-10 ELA-Literacy	RI.9-10.1 Cite strong and thorough textual evidence to support analysis of what the text says explicitly as well as inferences drawn from the text.
	RI.9-10.7 Analyze various accounts of a subject told in different mediums (e.g., a person's life story in both print and multimedia), determining which details are emphasized in each account.
	W.9-10.4 Produce clear and coherent writing in which the development, organization, and style are appropriate to task, purpose, and audience. (Grade-specific expectations for writing types are defined in standards 1–3 above.)
	W.9-10.9 Draw evidence from literary or informational texts to support analysis, reflection, and research.
	SL.9-10.1 Initiate and participate effectively in a range of collaborative discussions (one-on-one, in groups, and teacher-led) with diverse partners on grades 9–10 topics, texts, and issues, building on others' ideas and expressing their own clearly and persuasively.
	SL.9-10.2 Integrate multiple sources of information presented in diverse media or formats (e.g., visually, quantitatively, orally) evaluating the credibility and accuracy of each source.
	SL.9-10.4 Present information, findings, and supporting evidence clearly, concisely, and logically such that listeners can follow the line of reasoning and the organization, development, substance, and style are appropriate to purpose, audience, and task.
Grade 11-12 ELA-Literacy	RI.11-12.1 Cite strong and thorough textual evidence to support analysis of what the text says explicitly as well as inferences drawn from the text, including determining where the text leaves matters uncertain.
	RI.11-12.7 Integrate and evaluate multiple sources of information presented in different media or formats (e.g., visually, quantitatively) as well as in words in order to address a question or solve a problem.
	W.11-12.4 Produce clear and coherent writing in which the development, organization, and style are appropriate to task, purpose, and audience. (Grade-specific expectations for writing types are defined in standards 1–3 above.)
	W.11-12.9 Draw evidence from literary or informational texts to support analysis, reflection, and research.
	SL.11-12.1 Initiate and participate effectively in a range of collaborative discussions (one-on-one, in groups, and teacher-led) with diverse partners on grades 11–12 topics, texts, and issues, building on others' ideas and expressing their own clearly and persuasively.
	SL.11-12.2 Integrate multiple sources of information presented in diverse formats and media (e.g., visually, quantitatively, orally) in order to make informed decisions and solve problems, evaluating the credibility and accuracy of each source and noting any discrepancies among the data.
	SL.11-12.4 Present information, findings, and supporting evidence, conveying a clear and distinct perspective, such that listeners can follow the line of reasoning, alternative or opposing perspectives are addressed, and the organization, development, substance, and style are appropriate to purpose, audience, and a range of formal and informal tasks.

www.ingramcontent.com/pod-product-compliance
Ingram Content Group UK Ltd.
Pitfield, Milton Keynes, MK11 3LW, UK
UKHW012331270225
455677UK00027B/807